THE
VICTORY LAP
GROWING OLD WITH GOD

—BILLIE SILVEY—

21st Century Christian Publishing

ISBN: 978-0-89098-698-1

©2015 by 21st Century Christian

2809 12th Ave S, Nashville, TN 37204

All rights reserved.

Unless otherwise noted Scripture quotations are from the New International Version.

Scripture quotations taken from THE HOLY BIBLE, NEW INTERNATIONAL VERSION®, NIV®

Copyright © 1973, 1978, 1984, 2011 by Biblica, Inc.™

Used by permission. All rights reserved worldwide.

Cover design by Jonathan Edelhuber

Table of Contents

Introduction

I t was March 2012, and I was on the main campus of Westchester High School to pick up a student for counseling at our student services nonprofit, Westchester Healthy Start. In the nine years I'd worked for Healthy Start, I'd called countless students. But today, something was different; something was wrong.

My life was pretty routine—working part-time for Healthy Start, keeping house and spending time with my husband Frank, who had recently retired; our son, Robert, who had moved back in to help us with house payments when his apartment complex was razed; and our daughter, Kathy, and granddaughter, Katyana, who came to visit most Sundays after church.

Babysitting on occasion, publishing a monthly web magazine of articles I'd written to keep a hand in my "real" career—35 years as a writer and editor—fixing meals, doing laundry, visiting with friends, and worshipping each Sunday with the nearby Culver Palms Church of Christ made up the rest of my life.

Oh, I felt the odd stiffness and pain that seemed normal at the advanced age of 69, but that day I felt so weak that it was hard to pull myself up the stairs that connected our far-flung, multi-level campus. I glanced around quickly. Suddenly and without warning, I felt strangely disoriented. Where was I, and who was I coming to call out of class?

I panicked. I had to find out who I had come for and where she was, but my mind was a blank. Then I remembered. But it wasn't like a regular memory. It came slowly, like molasses on a cold day. I'd slipped the summons I'd written to call the student into my purse. It would tell me her name as well as the building and classroom she was in.

My hands trembled as I searched frantically for the yellow slip of paper. Yes, there it was, and there was her name. The slip also said what building and classroom she was in. Now if only I could find them. Eventually, I was able to pick her up and return to the office.

"We need to talk," I told Marvin, my boss, my mind a jumble of questions and concerns.

He looked at me closely. "Are you all right?"

"No, I'm not," I said. "Something is wrong."

"Take the rest of the day off if you're not feeling well. You can finish whatever you're working on in the morning."

Clearly I wasn't conveying the magnitude of the problem. "I need to go home," I told him, "but I may need a lot more time off than that."

It was obvious to me that suddenly I was not functioning; it seemed as if anybody could see it just by looking at me. "I need to make some doctors' appointments, have some tests run. Something is seriously wrong, and I need to find out what it is and what, if anything, can be done about it."

Something was wrong, but not even I knew how wrong until I'd struggled through brain surgery, a seizure, pneumonia, retirement, and my 70th birthday—all within a year.

Those experiences were like a splash of cold water in my face; I was growing old. In fact, I was already old. And my whole self—mind and body—seemed to be falling apart at the same time.

What I didn't expect was that it would impact my entire being—emotionally and spiritually—as well as my family and friends. And it would mean the end of my working life, which would bring adjustments of its own.

I had always been healthy, outgoing and happy. I had felt close to God and had even worked for a church. I had been bright and energetic, but I could hardly recognize the weak, stumbling, confused, and depressed old woman I had become. I wasn't even sure I liked her.

Some physical and mental difficulties are to be expected as we age. But they usually don't come quite so fast or so dramatically as they did with me.

But God's timing is perfect—so much more than I realized at the time. Medical science, particularly brain science, had progressed so far that problems could be diagnosed and treated that previously would have been dismissed as hopeless.

According to *The State of Aging and Health in America 2013*, a publication of the Centers for Disease Control and Prevention of the Department of Health and Human Service, "During the twentieth century, effective public health strategies and advances in medical treatment contributed to a dramatic increase in average life expectancy in the United States. The 30-year gain in life expectancy within the span of a century had never before been achieved. Many of the diseases that claimed our ancestors—including tuberculosis, diarrhea and enteritis, and syphilis—are no longer the threats they once were."

I started with our family doctor. He ran a few tests and referred me to a neurologist. She sent me for an MRI and for neurocognitive testing. When I went back for my follow-up appointment, she showed me pictures of slices of my brain. Even *I* could see that one ventricle was thinner than the other.

That, she explained, was the result of extra cerebrospinal fluid, which was putting pressure on my brain. The technical name for the condition was normal pressure hydrocephalus, and the symptoms included mental impairment and mobility problems. The diagnosis certainly fit my experience.

The neurologist referred me to a neurosurgeon, who placed a shunt in my skull to drain the excess fluid into my abdomen, where it could be absorbed.

Frank and I talked and figured and planned. What if it didn't go as advertised? What if this break from work became a permanent retirement? Taking a later-than-usual retirement meant that we had paid enough into Social Security and had sufficient pension funds to be able to live on our current income. Even turning 70 wasn't the unmitigated disaster it seemed at first.

Nevertheless, the challenges of aging that I experienced that year and the faith it's taken to find meaning, purpose and significance in my life led me to meditate, pray, and seek the counsel of strong Christian brothers and sisters.

Despite the kindness of the people around me, I felt old, useless, and weak. I was sure my life was over. I was complaining to my friend, Margaret, about what a failure I felt I was. Margaret is an elder's wife, the mother of four incredible daughters, a woman of wisdom, and one of the sweetest spirits I know. She said, "Don't look at it that way. This is your victory lap."

I looked up the phrase online. A victory lap is a term used in motor sports to describe an extra lap of the race track after the end of a race. Driven at reduced speed, it allows the winning driver to celebrate his or her victory and the spectators to congratulate and honor him or her.

I loved the image of a winner at the end of my race, taking some extra time to savor my accomplishments, to thank God and the people who contributed to making my life special, and to forgive those who didn't. It's an opportunity to enjoy myself in a way I hadn't been able to in the crush of family and career responsibilities.

I struggled through a year of recovering and listening to God's voice in everything from finding identity without a job title to strengthening muscles, rebuilding faith, and learning to trust a brain that had let me down. I even was able to share what I was learning by writing a Bible class curriculum on aging that I taught the following summer at the Culver Palms Church of Christ.

The class was called *Growing Old with God,* and it forms the basis of this book. There's an outline, together with instructions for using it for a class, in the back of this book. Mostly, it's for people like me who are confronting some of the difficulties that come with aging and seek, as I did, to be able to handle them with greater grace and joy. It discusses our need for a support network and how to grow one. It talks about our need to stay active and involved in life and shares ways to do that. It treats life and death and the legacy each of us is leaving for generations to come.

After all, I'm not the only one who's growing old. The whole population of the United States is aging rapidly. Our largest demographic, the Baby Boomers, the huge generation that follows mine, is retiring as well. I felt I had insights to share with a broader public.

The oldest baby boomers, those born between 1946 and 1964, started turning 65 in 2011. According to the U.S. Census Bureau, the number of people in the U.S. who are 65 and older is expected to more than double from 40 million to 89 million by 2050. By 2030, older adults will account for roughly twenty percent of the U.S. population.

Much has been said about finishing well. This is my victory lap, and I want to enjoy it—to regain a sense of myself and my purpose for still being here, to regain my peace and joy in Christ.

I pray that my experience and the lessons I've learned as a result of it will help you avoid some of the problems I've experienced and have a happier and more fulfilling victory lap. I pray that churches with aging populations will benefit from these discussions and from the contributions of their senior members, and that the older Christians will enjoy fuller lives and reduced distress at the prospect of aging.

CHAPTER 1

What Does It Mean to Grow Old?

I t's a Sunday morning. I wake up at 5:30—the usual time I get up these days. I no longer use an alarm clock but now wake up even earlier than I did with an alarm when I was working. I have hours before my daughter, Kathy, and granddaughter, Katyana, will pick me up for church.

A Bible verse is running through my head: "Establish the works of my hands" (Psalm 90:17). I ask God to continue bringing good from the work I've done over the years to serve Him and other people. Then I get up, unload the dish drainer, make coffee, and prepare breakfast.

I do the stretching exercises the physical therapist gave me when I was released from the hospital. I drink a big glass of water, write in my journal, and turn on the computer to check the weather—high of 71 and cloudy, which is about average for winter in Los Angeles.

I eat breakfast and am almost ready when Kathy drives up. A dab of lipstick, and we leave for worship several blocks away. There I meet with my brothers and sisters, sing, pray, laugh, and listen to a sermon and the reading of God's Word.

We come home and make sandwiches for lunch. I show Kathy the scrapbook I'm making of family photos. I'm writing blurbs to identify key people in the photos and to tell stories I recall about them. I want the kids and Katyana to have a family history—my side of the family and Frank's before there's no one left to recognize the people in the photos or to remember their stories.

Fortunately for me, Frank's mother felt much the same way. Before she died, she compiled photos and letters written by her family through the generations that supply the information I need about his side of the family. My sister is the historian on my side. She does extensive research and is a member of several genealogical societies. She shares a lot about the Wesleys, LaRoes, Huxfords and Hales—the four families that make up our genetic heritage.

We hear about the photo exhibit Kathy and Katyana went to the night before and see photos of some of the art they enjoyed.

Seven-year-old Katyana has brought home a yellow balloon from church, and we sit around the living room, trying to keep it aloft. Katyana chases around, working off excess energy. The rest of us sit until the balloon wobbles near, then whack it like a volleyball to one of the other family members.

After a spirited game, with lots of laughs and a few near misses of objects around the room, I show Kathy the recipes I made my grocery list from this week. She decides on a dish she'd like us to prepare. We go to the kitchen and work together on a Mexican casserole, then pop it in the oven, setting the timer for dinner. Katyana helps me set the table while it's cooking.

It's the good life.

The longer I live, the more important it becomes to live, not long, but well. The good life is a life of joy and gratitude, of learning and loving and being involved.

That's not the approach of our times. On television, commercials make it seem as if the important thing is to not show our age. The media tell us that we shouldn't want to look old. We need skin creams, hair dyes, and even facial surgery. Rather than respect older people, as is traditional in many cultures, our country has a negative view of age.

As a Christian, I feel it's important to be honest—to put forth the face I have to the world. I try to look decent, but not to hide the fact that I've been living and learning for a long time and just may have something to contribute.

Another set of commercials, for everything from walk-in bathtubs to home security systems, seems to want to frighten us. Our economy thrives on making people feel that they need to buy things to protect themselves from a dangerous world.

It is unnerving, even frightening, to grow old—especially when it seems as if you've suddenly become someone you don't recognize. It's not the way I'd ever seen myself before. I feel that our culture fails to respect me and other aging people for the contributions we have made—and still are making—to our society.

Most of the books I've read about aging emphasize finances. If you have enough money to constantly travel or redecorate your home, you'll be happy. Money is important for supplying our basic necessities, but generally, I feel that the value of money has been greatly exaggerated in our culture, and the value of intangibles like love and joy and peace has been overlooked. Those are what we need for the good life.

None of us is growing younger. We're all growing older, which comes with certain challenges. With prayer and preparation, we can respond to those challenges with strength, joy, and renewed purpose.

Age is relative. What's old to one person may not seem old to another. Think back over the older people in your life when you were growing up. Just how old were they? They may have been as young as 30 or as old as 60. A 60-year-old person that age doesn't seem so old now that I'm over 70.

Time is relative that way. Remember how long it took for Christmas to come when you were a child? Now it almost takes you by surprise.

Aging took me by surprise. It seemed as if I were just going along enjoying life when suddenly, I was old.

I had never felt particularly old until I got sick. I had always either been young or seemed young for my age. But the year I had major surgery, I wasn't able to pretend any more.

The day I got home from the hospital, I started home health care and watched a movie. Kathy and Katyana came over, and Kathy brushed out my hair, which a nurse had braided to keep it out of my face, and fixed dinner for Father's Day.

The next day, I watched another movie and called to make appointments with my family doctor, my neurologist, and my neurosurgeon, as I had been instructed me to do when I was released from the hospital.

Frank's brother called from Berkeley to see how I was doing. I told him I was doing so well that I knew I'd be back to normal in no time. I'm not sure whom I was trying to convince. I worked on my website, had sessions with my home health nurse and physical therapist, shampooed my hair, and watched yet another movie. (Obviously, I saw a lot of movies.)

Kathy was speaking at a conference for English professors up the coast in Monterey. We planned to tag along and keep Katyana while Kathy was in sessions. I encouraged Frank to go ahead with them. Our son, Robert, would be here to help me if I needed anything.

Then on Saturday, I had a seizure. Robert called 911, and I ended up back in the hospital for a second week. Frank and Kathy were on their way home when Robert reached them with the news.

A month later, I got up after the best sleep I'd had in weeks then worked on my website links and a grocery list. Frank made breakfast, and I started writing in the new journal Kathy had given me for Christmas. Its cover was the softest leather, and it had a picture of the Trevi Fountain in Rome on it. The pages were cool, smooth, and easy to write on.

I thanked God for the good care the doctors and nurses had

given me. I thanked Him for both my family and my church family and asked blessings on each one. "I ask this of You who is God alone, the great Unutterable One, the Incomprehensible One, to Whom all governments are subject and every authority bows, before Whom all that is high falls down and remains silent, at whose voice demons take flight and beholding Whom all creation surrenders in silent adoration," I prayed.

The next day a neighbor brought me a bunch of yellow roses, and the florist delivered a fruit and flower basket from friends at church. A few days later, another friend came with lasagna for our dinner. And one of the elders of my church emailed that he'd probably stop by the next evening.

The appraiser was coming to look at our house that morning, and the physical therapist was scheduled for another session. I bathed and got ready for them. I prayed for friends who were ill and for two who had been recently widowed. The elder came by, and one of our ministers made a short visit.

Despite the good things that were happening, the time just after I came home from the hospital was filled with emotional ups and downs, encouragements and discouragements, a sense of being close to God and simultaneously feeling alienated.

Because of my illness, I was forced to retire. I'd always enjoyed my work, so I didn't eagerly await retirement as some people do. I didn't know what to do with myself. In fact, I wasn't sure just who "myself" was.

It was around this time, when I was feeling low and full of

self-doubt, that my friend, Margaret christened this period as my "victory lap." The phrase caused something to break loose in my mind. There *was* good here. I was having trouble seeing it, but I started looking more closely. It was a chance to celebrate, to accept congratulations, and to finish stronger. A new, more biblically based way of looking at age, it was the first step in my year-long process of changing my attitude, and as a result, my capabilities.

It meant that, in a sense, my race was over. Jesus had won it on my behalf when I obediently accepted Him in faith. "Thanks be to God. He gives us the victory through our Lord Jesus Christ" (1 Corinthians 15:57).

It reminded me of the words of the writer to the Hebrews: "Therefore, since we are surrounded by such a great cloud of witnesses, let us throw off everything that hinders and the sin that so easily entangles, and let us run with perseverance the race marked out for us" (Hebrews 12:1). That writer pictures our lives as a cosmic race.

When I began writing this book, the 2014 Winter Olympics were taking place in Sochi, Russia. Vast crowds were watching as athletes pushed themselves to do their personal best.

To the writer of Hebrews, the crowds who observe our performance in the race of life are all the faithful who have gone before us who are listed in Hebrews 11—Abel, Enoch, Noah, Abraham, Sarah, Isaac, Jacob, Joseph, Moses, the Israelites, Rahab, the judges, King David, and the prophets and martyrs.

With such an audience looking on, we want to free ourselves

from entanglements like sins, worries, and material things, so we may finish the race of our life well.

One night, Frank and I watched the downhill skiing competition held at the Rosa Khutor Mountain Ski Center on the Aibga Ridge. The Olympic Alpine skiing routes total 3,500 meters in length, with a 46 degree slope. The Center accommodates 18,000 spectators.

We saw the blue lines on the course in which the skiers had to stay inside as they flew down the course, as high as three Empire State Buildings at speeds over 80 mph, making football-field-length jumps. The best idea most of us may have of what it's like to ski the course is to watch former Olympic skier and BBC commentator Gordon Bell, who skied it without poles but with a hand-held camera.[1]

Our course, like that of the skiers, has been set before us. God knows the limits of our lives. He's set the boundaries, like those blue lines between which the skiers have to stay. I was getting ahead of myself, deciding that I was useless, that I was dying. As long as we're alive, God has a purpose for us. Our part is merely to get rid of anything that would obstruct us in our flight—greed, jealousy, bitterness, immorality, lack of peace, or lack of love—and to patiently trust Him to reveal that course to us.

"Let us fix our eyes on Jesus, the author and perfecter of our faith, who for the joy set before him endured the cross, scorning its shame, and sat down at the right hand of the throne of God" (Hebrews 12:2).

Though it's important to read the Old Testament for context

and the epistles for practical guidance, the heart of Scripture is the Gospels: Matthew, Mark, Luke and John. Those are the four accounts of Jesus' life as a person here on earth.

Jesus is our example of the perfect life of faith, and if we keep His example before us as we live, we can't go wrong. "Consider him who endured such opposition from sinful men, so that you will not grow weary and lose heart" (Hebrews 12:3).

Though our lives may not be all we'd like them to be, though weariness and discouragement may challenge us, we haven't faced all that He did. "In your struggle against sin, you have not yet resisted to the point of shedding your blood. And you have forgotten that word of encouragement that addresses you as sons:

"My son, do not make light of the Lord's discipline,
And do not lose heart when he rebukes you,
Because the Lord disciplines those he loves,
And he punishes everyone he accepts as a son."'

~ Hebrews 12:4-6

The challenges that confront us are a part of God's discipline of us, His children, aimed at strengthening us and preparing us for the long haul. "No discipline seems pleasant at the time," the writer tells us. "Later on, however, it produces a harvest of righteousness and peace for those who have been trained by it" (Hebrews 12:11).

Olympic athletes are among the best in the world. They have been trained and encouraged by coaches to be strong, nimble, and flexible so they can turn in stellar performances. God is our coach. He's not some stern judge watching from Heaven, hoping to catch us doing something wrong. He's our loving coach who trains and encourages us and wants the best for us. "Therefore strengthen your feeble arms and weak knees. Make level paths for your feet, so that the lame may not be disabled, but rather healed" (Hebrews 12:13).

I had almost given up on the race too early. I had lost sight of the possibility of healing. But that was what God had in store for me. Though I've learned since that a year is about average for healing after brain surgery, it would take the longest year of my life, but healing did come.

Jesus has already accomplished our victory. We have merely to accept what He's done for us by faith and to continue in that faith until the end. Spiritual growth is a process that should continue throughout our lives to the extent that the oldest among us is the most spiritual, most loving, most joyous, most open, patient, and kind person of all. She should be willing to listen, learn, and change. He should be compassionate, single-hearted, pure, and peaceful.

What is your concept of age? "What we think about a person influences how we will perceive him; how we perceive him influences how we will behave toward him; and how we behave toward him ultimately shapes who he is," sociologists Kenneth J. and Mary M. Gergen write in the Social Gerontology of Aging.[2]

We can have a bad self image if we let others set it for us. Many people today go through life primarily in the company of others their own age. The young and old rarely have meaningful interactions outside of the family. Therefore, many have a stereotypical view of older people.

That view may resemble Maxine from greeting card fame and pop culture: negative and miserable. Here are some typical Maxine-isms: [3]

"I'm going South for the winter," she says. "Actually some parts of me are headed there already."

"Don't let aging get you down. It's too hard to get back up!"

There are negative aspects to aging, and we can concentrate on them if we insist. We can moan, complain, and turn into cranky old men and women.

Maxine does, however, say several things that are helpful:

"If you woke up breathing, congratulations. You have another chance." She's certainly right there. So long as we're alive, we have a chance to make something of the time God has given us.

"Inside every older person is a younger person wondering what happened." Perhaps the most surprising thing to me about aging is realizing how little I seem to have changed inside. I still *feel* young, despite the way I look and the number of birthdays I've celebrated.

That is Maxine, and her view of aging represents that of many people today. But what does the Bible say about age? In the class

I taught, I distributed strips of paper with Bible verses on them. The passages for this lesson were Job 12:12, Psalm 92:12-14, Proverbs 16: 31, Isaiah 46:3-4 and Titus 2:1-5. Each person in the class who had one read it and explained what the passage was saying about age.

The passage from Job says, "Is not wisdom found among the aged? Does not long life bring understanding?" (Job 12:12). I had always thought so, but now the brain that I had counted on seemed compromised. What did that mean for the wisdom and understanding I was supposed to have accumulated through the years? Maybe I just had to trust God's Word, even when it didn't seem that way to me.

The Psalmist writes: "The righteous will flourish like a palm tree, they will grow like a cedar of Lebanon; planted in the house of the Lord, they will flourish in the courts of our God. They will still bear fruit in old age, they will stay fresh and green" (Psalm 92:12-14). Having grown up in the dry climate of West Texas, I understood that one. It recalls the freshness of rain after dry, dusty heat. With God's help, I still might have some freshness in me.

The wise man wrote in Proverbs: "Gray hair is a crown of splendor; it is attained by a righteous life" (Proverbs 16:31). Years ago, I determined not to color my hair, but to let it gray naturally. I tend to be a natural person. I had my kids naturally, breast-fed, and trusted God that everything would work as advertised. I haven't been disappointed on that count so far, so I should resist temptation now, and enjoy my crown of silver.

But most significant to me were Isaiah's words: "Listen to me, O house of Jacob, all you who remain of the house of Israel, you whom I have upheld since you were conceived, and have carried since your birth. Even to your old age and gray hairs I am he, I am he who will sustain you. I have made you and will carry you; I will sustain you and I will rescue you" (Isaiah 46:3-4).

God will take care of me. He will sustain and carry and rescue me in this final part of my life as He has through the rest of it.

I grew up in the little church in Happy, Texas, with Maude Bowe as my Bible class teacher. Ms. Bowe emphasized learning Scripture. I went to the public school there with Lela Foster Moudy as an English teacher who gave extra credit for outside reading. She gave me extra credit for reading through the Bible when I was in high school.

I studied the Bible in college, first at Abilene Christian and then at Pepperdine. Then I worked for *20th Century Christian Magazine,* where I was thrilled to discover that I could be paid to study Scripture. Their wording still flits through my mind on almost any subject.

The God that I met in Scripture was the God I had given myself to in baptism when I was 13—the one I had talked with in my prayers. He had sustained me throughout my life, and I knew that He would continue to sustain me. He would make sense of the pain and confusion, the sorrow and loss. He would help me find the victory in these, the waning years of my life.

Paul, writing to Titus in the second chapter of his epistle, says:

"You must teach what is in accord with sound doctrine. Teach the older men to be temperate, worthy of respect, self-controlled, and sound in faith, in love and in endurance. Likewise, teach the older women to be reverent in the way they live, not to be slanderers or addicted to much wine, but to teach what is good. Then they can train the younger women to love their husbands and children, to be self-controlled and pure, to be busy at home, to be kind, and to be subject to their husbands, so that no one will malign the word of God" (Titus 2:1-5).

I am deeply grateful as I look back over a life spent teaching children, women, and even some men through my writing and speaking engagements at women's retreats and college lectureships all over the country. I have had wonderful opportunities to teach what is good. I have trained younger women to love their husbands and children, both in word and by example.

The high point of my time since my surgery came when Frank and I celebrated our 50th wedding anniversary. After a rocky start, we learned to love each other increasingly as the years went by.

One thing that made our marriage work is that Frank is interesting and principled. I've enjoyed being married to him, and I've learned a lot from him. A good and loving husband and father, he has encouraged and supported me in everything I've attempted—and does to this day.

So much of our experience of age depends on our attitude. It depends on our definition of the good life. Is it money, position, looks? These can, and usually do, fail. Is it joy and relationships and staying close to God? These never fail.

In our Bible class, we wrote in our journals about our childhoods and the older people who impacted our lives. I wrote about my paternal grandmother, Granny, Ethel Wesley. When I was a child, Granny probably made the greatest impact on me of any older person. She took me to church before my parents began attending.

She was interested in everything, and she read a lot—especially the Bible and *National Geographic* magazines. She was interested in outer space and always wanted to go there.

She was creative and made things such as braided rag rugs, quilts, crocheted and knitted work, and her own clothes. She made candles and soap and decorated mirrors and other items with sea shells. She also had a plum tree and a large garden filled with flowers and vegetables, the harvest of which she used to can and make jelly.

I vividly remember the day I saw a tarantula at the side of her house, between the fence and the road. Granny got a jelly jar and punched holes in the top of it with a hammer and nail. Then she squatted down and jumped along behind that tarantula until she'd caught it with a special direction to me, "for you to take to school for science class."

I was scared, but Granny was fearless.

Just as Granny blessed my life in her later years, God gives each of us who is still alive a victory lap. How can we express our gratitude to Him for that special gift? How can we not waste it?

How can we use that extra time He's given us to glorify Him and to help others?

I am learning to treasure my victory lap by looking back over my life with gratitude to God and the people who made it possible and pleasant, and forgiving those who didn't; praying to God to bring good from it—to "establish the work of my hands," and to forgive the wrong I've done and wash it away in Jesus' blood; and continuing to do what I'm able—writing this book, maintaining my website, collecting family photos and stories for my children and grandchild, and praying for those in need. Among these endeavors, I try to be alert to other possibilities for service.

Others my age may not be able to do all these things, and there are plenty of things I can't do. We need to accept our limitations and do what we're able. Even if we're bedridden, we can pray. Prayer has tremendous power. We can count our blessings; gratitude helps lift our spirits. And we can encourage someone else who may not have it as easy as we do.

What does it mean to grow old? It means a lot. It means that you'll experience limitations you've never known before. It means that other people will look at you in ways they never have before. It means that you'll have less energy than you're used to having. It means that you'll remember some things with remarkable clarity, but may not be able to recall something that happened yesterday.

And it doesn't mean so much. You're still basically the same person you've always been, with the same strengths and weaknesses. You feel much the same way—no better, though often not a lot worse. You have less energy, but you're willing to let more things go because you realize that all those things that always seemed so urgent aren't really all that pressing.

You're more accepting—with yourself and other people. You have a clearer sense of what's important and what really isn't.

I may not appreciate the attitudes those around me have about age, but I don't worry about others' opinions as much as I once did. I'm grateful for the work that's been done toward equal treatment without regard to age, but I try to show by the way I live that I deserve to be treated with respect.

As I do that, I find my attitude about age changing. I don't think so much about what I *can't* do as about what I *can*, and I am grateful. I take my eyes off myself and focus on Jesus and others. Life is still pretty good—even though I'm growing old, I'm retired, and physically and mentally I'm not what I once was.

What I am is God's child. With my eyes on Jesus and the victory He's won for me, I can finish the race that is set before me with patient trust and confidence. When everything seemed to fall apart, it was an opportunity to consider how I wanted to reconstruct my life. So now, at age 71, I'm just beginning to live the good life, to enjoy my victory lap.

Discussion Questions

1. How has your concept of what it means to be old changed over the years?

2. What age seemed old when you were younger? What does now?

3. When did you first become aware of being old? What prompted it?

4. For what and whom in your past are you grateful? Whom do you need to forgive? Make plans to do that. If the person is no longer living, turn the situation over to God in prayer, and trust Him to handle it on your behalf.

5. What's the difference between the way you look on the outside and the way you feel inside?

6. What advantages might there be to aging?

Bible Study

1. "Is not _____ found among the aged? Does not long life bring _____ " (Job 12:12).

2. "The righteous will flourish like a _____ _____, they will grow like a _____ of Lebanon; planted in the house of the Lord, they will _____ in the courts of our God. They will still bear _____ in old age, they will stay _____ and _____ " (Psalm 92:12-14).

3. "_____ _____ is a crown of splendor; it is attained by a _____ life" (Proverbs 16:31).

4. "Listen to me, Oh house of Jacob, all you who remain in the house
of Israel, you whom I have _____ since you were

_____, and have _____

since your birth. Even to your _____ _____

and _____ _____ I am he who will

_____ you. I have _____

you and will _____ you and I will

_____ you" (Isaiah 46:3-4).

5. "Teach the older men to be _____, worthy

of _____, _____ and

sound in _____, in _____ and

in _____." And teach the older women

to be _____ in the way they live,

not to be _____ or addicted

to _____ _____, but to teach what is

_____. Then they can train the younger

women to _____ their husbands and children,

to be _____ and _____, to be

_____ at home, to be _____, and to be

_____ to their husbands so that no one will malign

the word of God" (Titus 2:1-5).

Write in Your Journal

Write in your journal about an older person who made a deep impression on you as a child. Who was it? What did that person do? What does that tell you about growing older and how to use your victory lap to glorify God and help other people?

Endnotes

1 http://www.cbssports.com/olympics/eye-on-olympics/24437377/video-see-what-its-like-to-ski-sochi-downhill-course.

2 https://www.trinity.edu/mkearl/gersopsy.html.

3 http://www.hallmark.com/online/maxine/about/.

CHAPTER 2

What Are the Challenges of Retirement?

There are many challenges to growing old: physical, mental, emotional, spiritual. These are the topics of chapters to follow. Individual people will have trouble with different challenges, but retirement itself turned out to be the greatest challenge for me.

Work had always been important to me. I had allowed it to become more tangled than it should have been with my identity. I was a writer. I was an editor. I was a nonprofit manager.

I had started working in 1950 when my dad bought the *Happy Herald*, the weekly newspaper in Happy, Texas. Happy had a population of just 642, and I always joked that it was 641 after I left for college. But through the '50s, I wrote articles, sold ads, set type, ran presses, and swept floors for my dad. I dreamed that I was Lois Lane, girl journalist.

When I graduated from high school in 1961, I attended West Texas State University and then moved to Abilene and started writing publicity for Abilene Christian College, now ACU. Frank and I married in 1963, and I edited the *Optimist*, the student newspaper, in 1964. When we transferred to Pepperdine in 1965,

I began writing publicity for them.

I enjoyed writing, and it came easy for me.

In 1971, I started writing and editing for *20th Century Christian* publishing company, working for them through the next twenty-five years. That's what I consider my real career—planning issues, assigning articles, editing copy, choosing art and planning layouts for the monthly religious journal.

I also wrote a series of Bible study books—*God Has a Plan for You, God Has a Savior for You, God has a Mission for You*—each based on a different book of the New Testament. I loved the fact that I could be paid to study the Bible, which I enjoyed doing anyway.

As the books sold, I was invited to speak for various church groups and college lecture series and was interviewed on Christian radio. That allowed me to travel, to get to know wonderful Christians all over the country, and to get to know parts of the country that were new to me.

Even the radio interviews were interesting, though I tended to get nervous, not knowing what questions I might be asked. I enjoyed reading over my work, laying out the book and a glass of water, box of tissues and package of cough drops on the desk, and waiting for the phone to ring. Most of my interviews were by phone, though one was in a local studio.

By the mid-'90s, however, I was feeling less satisfied with my career in Christian journalism. It was evident that I'd hit a glass ceiling and had nowhere to go professionally. Beyond that, I was frustrated with the lack of feedback. I wrote and edited from my home and sent the issues to our headquarters in Nashville, Tennessee, but any reader response was directed there, not to me. I had no clue how many people, if any, were reading my work, much less if it was helpful to them.

The work was perfect when our children were young. I could edit and watch them at the same time. But as they grew, I found it lonely to work by myself with no colleagues. I decided to find an area of service that would allow me to work more directly with other people.

In 1995, I was hired by the Culver Palms Church of Christ in Los Angeles to work in outreach and involvement. For the next eight years, I wrote publicity, created ads and flyers, and started Life Skills Lab, a job training program for single parents.

Life Skills Lab was the most satisfying challenge I'd ever attempted. Every day afforded me contact with students, prospective students, teachers, volunteers, agency personnel and supporters, as well as local political, educational and religious leaders. At times it seemed as if there was nothing but feedback: complaints, needs, constant demands. It required every ounce of my creativity, skills, and effort just to keep it going.

Then, in 2003, Life Skills Lab closed for lack of money. I felt like such a failure! It had been my responsibility to bring in the funding needed to keep it afloat, and I hadn't been able to do it. I realized that I should have prepared myself better by studying business and nonprofit management. I should have prepared the church better to see the connection between being a Christian and helping people. And I should have made sure that our board realized that our primary aim was to help people get jobs, not help employers get employees.

I was happy that we had helped some people but sad to realize that we could have helped so many more. The need for jobs is never just a one-time thing. Life Skills Lab ended before the big financial downturn of 2008, when so many people needed help finding employment.

But God was good, as He always is. He provided me with a position with Westchester Healthy Start, a student services program on the campus of Westchester High School. Working with urban high school students presented its own set of challenges, but it, too, was rewarding. That was where I was working when my illness forced me to retire in Spring of 2012. By that point, I'd been working for more than 60 years.

At first, retirement wasn't easy for me. I felt depressed without the structure of a job and the satisfaction of being able to help people. In fact, according to Sarah Bercier, a Retirement Planning Institute resource specialist from Canada, approximately thirty percent of workers have at least temporary trouble adjusting to retirement. These problems can continue for a few months or even years.[4]

Retired women suffer greater rates of depression than retired men — roughly fourteen percent of women compared with seven percent of men. However, "rates for male suicide spike significantly after [age] 65," Bercier says, "to almost triple the rate of the general population."

Symptoms of depression—fatigue, lack of appetite, minor aches and pains, and problems concentrating—may be mistaken for signs of normal aging, so they may not be addressed. Sufferers should seek professional help, either medical help or counseling. I sought counseling from our minister. I also received support from my family, and guidance from God's Word.

Retirement was one of the most difficult adjustments of my life. Until then, I knew who I was—a working wife and mother, a writer, and an editor. I was accustomed to deadlines, to having to juggle my responsibilities and manage my time. Suddenly, it was all gone.

I had nothing but time. The only deadline I had was to put up my website on the last night of each month so it would be there for anyone seeking it the next morning. Thanks to my family, I managed to keep that deadline. Even when I was in the hospital, Kathy brought her laptop, and we finished one website entry on my bed. She thought it was crazy, but she did it, and I was grateful.

It was our assistant minister, Ron Cox, who first suggested that retirement might have been harder on me than I'd realized. He came to visit me when I got home from the hospital. I told him that I was having trouble with depression, and when he realized that I had only been retired for six months, he suggested that it might not be the surgery, but the retirement that was making me depressed. I told him that I'd always had problems with my identity being too closely tied to what I did.

He reminded me that God holds my identity. God knows who I am and who I am supposed to be. I need to trust him and pray that he'll reveal to me who he wants me to be and what he wants me to do. My body and my brain were already beginning to heal, but that was the beginning of the healing of my personality.

Work is a part of God's plan for us, His people. It began with creation, when God "took the man and put him in the Garden of Eden to work it and take care of it" (Genesis 2:15).

It keeps us occupied, hence the word *occupation*. "As long as it is day, we must do the work of him who sent me. Night is coming, when no one can work" (John 9:4).

It keeps us involved with our own business and out of other people's: "Make it your ambition to lead a quiet life, to mind your own business and to work with your hands, just as we told you" (1 Thessalonians 4:11). It makes us respectable, contributing members of society: "So that your daily life may win the respect of outsiders and so that you will not be dependent on anybody" (1 Thessalonians 4:12).

Financial compensation is a nice extra, and we need it to live, but we also need something to occupy our minds and our hands. Work is one way we interact with the world. It's important to me to add my contribution to that of all those who work to make life full and complete for everyone. It's a way of contributing our skills to help others and of thanking all those people who've contributed to us—teachers, grocers, law enforcement officers, ministers, authors, garment workers, and artists to name a few.

God had put me in positions of service throughout my life, first working for my dad, then in Christian education and Christian journalism, and finally in nonprofit management. I enjoyed stretching myself to solve problems, working with people to promote good, and helping others succeed.

A couple of years after Life Skills Lab ended, I began to realize that I was missing the discipline and structure of deadlines. All my life, I'd had them. My dad's newspaper had one every week. That seemed excessive, but the monthly schedule at *20th Century Christian* seemed just about right. How could I reincorporate that schedule into my life?

In July of 2005, I began writing four articles on a topic I was just discovering—church planting. I interviewed a friend who was involved in this ministry of starting churches in areas where the church is weak. My husband Frank helped me with the technical part, and we subscribed to a reasonable service through our email providers. We published the articles online at *billiesilvey. com*, and I was up and running.

I described my emagazine as "an eclectic website about women, Christianity, history, culture and the arts—and anything else that comes to mind." I've written about a variety of topics, including mystery novels, time, architecture, travel, the Depression, the environment, geography, science, and food.

I send out monthly notices to friends and family, but I also hear from teachers who use my various websites in classroom projects.

It's great for me. I'm constantly learning new facts as I research the various issues. I'm still a writer, pushing myself to produce interesting articles and find the right words to tell the story. It helps me keep up with technology as I lay out the pages and choose images and colors to illustrate them. And I have a deadline again. The last night of each month, I put up an entirely new issue.

At least eighty percent of older people plan to work at least part-time during retirement. And work doesn't have to be something for which you're paid. If you don't need the income of a paid profession, there are opportunities for volunteer service.

Work was formalized in the Ten Commandments: "Six days you shall labor and do all your work, but the seventh day is a Sabbath to the Lord your God" (Exodus 20:9-10). With children, a job, personal writing, teaching and volunteering, I wasn't always able to confine my labor to six days, but I always set aside time for worship on the Lord's Day and for devotions through the week.

God inspired the craftsmen Bezalel and Oholiab to do the work of building and furnishing the tabernacle and making garments for the priests (Exodus 31:1-11). I pray often for inspiration and to be used to inspire and help others.

When David, the king, returned to Jerusalem after putting down Absalom's rebellion, his 80-year-old advisor, Barzillai, came to cross the Jordan with him before returning to his home. When David invited Barzillai to come with him so he could care for him, Barzillai explained that at his age, he had lost discrimination, taste, and hearing. He would be a burden to the king and wanted only to return to his home to die (2 Samuel 19:34-37).

That was much the way I felt after I was ill, retired, and had turned 70. I felt I had nothing to contribute and would only be a burden to others.

Much of my problem was one of identity. We aren't just what we do. As important as work is, I need to be careful not to confuse what I *do* with who I *am*. I may be a writer, but that's not my identity. My real self is much more complex, a combination of body, mind, and spirit, of ligaments and synapses, of past and present, memories and activities, of relationships with people and with my father, God.

It was as the psalmist says:

The length of our days is seventy years—
　　Or eighty, if we have the strength;
yet their span is but trouble and sorrow,
　　for they quickly pass, and we fly away.
　　　　　　　　　　　～ Psalm 90:10

* * *

I had forgotten the prayer of the psalmist:

Since my youth, O God, you have taught me,
　　And to this day I declare your marvelous deeds.
Even when I am old and gray,
　　Do not forsake me, O God
Till I declare your power to the next generation,

Your might to all who are to come.

~ Psalm 71:17-18

* * *

May the favor of the Lord our God rest upon us;

Establish the work of our hands for us—

Yes, establish the work of our hands.

~ Psalm 90:17

The psalmist wants God to be with him in his old age. He promises to continue worshipping and serving if God will remain with him and establish the work of his hands or let the good that he's done remain effective. That was what I made my prayer: "'Establish the work of my hands.' Let good come from the sixty years I've been working. Let faith grow from the seeds I've planted in the minds of others over those years, despite the fact that I'm no longer gainfully employed."

And here, too, God has been faithful. I have often been surprised when someone reminds me of something I've written or said in a Bible class that was helpful to them. I rejoice that God has established my work, despite my shortcomings.

I have a beautiful quilt trimmed with shades of turquoise, rust, and olive that lies on top of my bed. It was designed and made by Christian women in Albuquerque, New Mexico. They had read my story about Granny and how she used scraps of fabric to make things of beauty. The quilt features the Storyteller *kachina* doll with children tumbling over her. She represents me and the stories I tell in my writing. Around the edges are stitched scenes from New Mexico ranging from an Indian *adobe* to baskets to hot air balloons.

The women who made it gave it to me when I spoke for a retreat there, and it's one of my most treasured possessions.

The teacher who wrote Ecclesiastes says, "Remember your Creator in the days of your youth." He follows with a figurative description of old age, urging us to "remember" before it's too late, and to "fear God and keep his commandments" (Ecclesiastes 12).

The members of the class I taught about aging wrote in their journals about their employment histories, the paid and volunteer work they've done, how they've defined themselves, and how that definition is changing as they grow older.

Additionally, I wrote about volunteering with the March of Dimes and the American Heart Association as a high school student. I wrote about working with the church wherever I found myself—teaching Bible classes, doing fundraising projects, serving in ministries for the homeless, and working on the benevolence committee. I also worked with my kids' schools when they were younger and more recently, with city and county government on children's and neighborhood planning councils.

As Os Guinness wrote in *The Call*: "We may retire from our jobs, but there's no retiring from our individual callings. We may cut back from our public responsibilities, but there is no cutting back from our corporate calling as the people of God. Above all, we may reach the place where we can see the end of the road, but our eyes are then to be fixed more closely on the one at the end of the road who is Father and home."[5]

After our Bible class discussed the journal assignment, Ron Halbert spoke as our guest expert. Ron is an M.D. and consultant who teaches at the School of Public Health at UCLA. He pointed out that our society doesn't have a good model for *senescence,* for growing old. "Our model, in this country, is of growth and improvement. But by age 30, our physical abilities begin to diminish. We don't have a good mental map or model for gracious aging."

"For some people, pretending helps," Ron said. "But pretending works just so long. Eventually we have to face the reality of aging."

I realized how true that was, and how I needed a plan for my own life—whether there was a lot or only a little of it left. I already had my website, and I determined to turn my Bible class on aging and the things I had learned from my experiences into a book. That gave me two writing projects to alternate each day.

Ron talked about the fact that our bodies are designed to be used. "Losing ability doesn't mean giving up. We have tons of evidence for the principle of 'use it or lose it.' Senescence, or loss of function, doesn't mean that we shouldn't be active. Our bodies are very eager and respond well to activity—cardiovascular, strength training, exercise—until we die."

He gave the example of a researcher who put people in a nursing home on a weight training regimen. They did leg extensions with even small weights and found a fifty percent increase in muscle strength in their quads, the fronts of their thighs.

If we stay still, those muscles atrophy quickly, but if we exercise, strength returns rapidly. A fifty percent improvement is the difference between being able to stand without assistance and not.

"Movement is life," Ron says. "Even in decline, we need to have a mental model so we don't get discouraged and quit moving. In earlier years, when people quit working, they just went home and sat. Now we realize that that is just the wrong thing to do."

We recently became very active preparing to host Katyana's friends at a party for her eighth birthday. We worked on the outside of the house. Frank finished his project of repainting the trim, and we filled in the flower bed and cleaned the yard. We also cleaned inside the house and painted a little. We enjoyed hosting ten excited children who helped us stay young and were grateful for the preparation, which helped us keep working.

"At one point, age was used to determine whether a person qualified for surgery," Ron told us. "Now age doesn't disqualify anybody. It's more a question of what you were doing yesterday that you could be doing tomorrow after treatment.

"Being active after an acute event—from a broken hip to a heart attack—can improve our level of function. There's a real danger in just lying on your back," he said, explaining why nurses want patients to be mobile so quickly after procedures.

My own experience proved that Ron was right. The nurses

pushed me to move while I was in the hospital, and now I was planning all sorts of interesting projects to keep me moving—and thinking and growing. I am so grateful that the doctors hadn't decided I was too old to bother operating on. If your doctor seems to think you are, you might want to look for another doctor.

"Movement is important for several reasons," Ron pointed out. "One is flexibility, the number one thing that keeps us from getting hurt. Also, balance and coordination, which prevent falls. Falls can cause breaks in the hip, the humerus (shoulder or upper arm), the wrist and/or the ankle. When we reject the out-of-work-retire-and-die pattern, we'll find we can preserve a lot of function."

Preserving function is not the same as staying young. "To see it as a way of staying young is not useful," Ron says. "That devalues the wisdom and experience of age."

"We need a mental model that incorporates death," he continued. "Americans want to pretend that people don't die. A healthy mental map understands that there is an end. Every year is precious at the end of life. Don't give up too quickly."

Life is a blessing, and it's a blessing to be used to bless others. Ask God what He has in mind for you in these precious later years of life. Ask Him to show you who He wants you to be and what He wants you to do. Take all the aspects of aging that represent challenges to you and lay them out before Him. He already knows, but it isn't communication until you know, too, and are able to share those challenges with Him.

Don't try to come off looking better than you are. He knows all about you—and He loves you anyway. Be honest, be yourself, be real. God made you, and He honors you as His creation.

Talk with Christian friends about the challenges you face, and ask for their prayers. "Therefore confess your sins to each other and pray for each other so that you may be healed. The prayer of a righteous man is powerful and effective" (James 5:16).

I have found this to be true as I've confessed, not just sins, but weaknesses and problems, to Christian brothers and sisters. They've prayed, and the problem has either been removed or improved, or I've made peace with it.

The challenges of retirement are many. First, don't confuse your life with your working life. Just because you've retired doesn't mean your life is over. It also doesn't mean that you don't still have work to do.

God has a plan for your life—for all of it. He has work for you to do until you die. The fact that you're alive means you still have purpose. It may be related to the work you did on the job, or it may be totally different.

Second, you still need to fill your time with useful effort. You need to be occupied even if you no longer have an occupation.

Ask God what He has in mind for you. Look over your work and volunteer history for particular skills you can contribute to those around you.

You can read and watch TV, but you can also do things that are more challenging to you and helpful to others.

Some people get another job. Some apply their skills to volunteer work. I enjoy a looser combination of set tasks and special projects, broken by free time so I can take advantage of opportunities that arise such as spending time with family and friends, learning new things, doing things I particularly enjoy as well as things that are others-centered.

Being retired made it possible for us to accept the invitation from one of Frank's brothers to spend a week at a villa outside of Rome one summer. We were able to stop off for a weekend in Paris on the way home, just because our granddaughter wanted to visit France. That kind of flexibility is precious.

During my victory lap, I look back with appreciation on the opportunities I've had to be of service in the past. I think of all the things I've learned, the new people I've come to know, and the experiences I've enjoyed during my working life. Now that I'm retired, I look forward with anticipation to areas of service God has planned for me in the future. (He must be keeping me around for something.) I determine to do what I can now to continue serving, to encourage others, to share my thoughts and concerns, and to pray for myself and for others who are experiencing challenges during their victory laps.

Discussion Questions

1. What was your career when you were working?

2. In what volunteer efforts have you participated?

3. What skills did you develop when you were working/volunteering?

4. What were the greatest challenges/rewards of work/volunteering?

5. How did (do) you feel about retirement?

6. What are the greatest challenges of aging for you?

Bible Study

1. What is the first example of work in the Bible?

2. What does the Law of Moses say about work?

3. What two craftsmen did God inspire for creative work on the tabernacle? (Exodus 31:1-11). What can you seek inspiration to do?

4. Who had worked with King David but was ready to retire? (2 Samuel 19:34-37). Are you ready to retire? How can you get ready?

5. What are some of the messages from the book of Psalms about age and work? (Psalms 90:10; 71:17-18; 90:17).

Write in Your Journal

Write in your journal about your employment history — the paid and volunteer work that you've done. Include how God guided and helped you get work and do your work, and how He brought people into your life to help you and that you could help.

Endnotes

4 http://www.rpi-ipr.com/pssa/en/newsletter/2011/2/news_short.
cfm?year=2011&month=2&item=2.

5 Os Guinness, The Call: Finding and Fulfilling the Central Purpose of Your Life.
(Nashville, TN.: Word Publishing, 1998), pp. 241-2,

CHAPTER 3

How Can We Maintain Our Physical Health?

When I was released from the hospital, I was assigned a home health care nurse and a physical therapist who came to our house. The nurse was hopeless. She'd ask me how I was doing, but wouldn't wait for me to answer. She seemed to feel like she was on the radio and had to avoid dead air time. She spent all her time talking about various members of *her* family and what *they* had experienced as they grew older, no matter how different their experiences were from mine. She talked to me like I was a five-year-old—or in the advanced stages of Alzheimer's. Maybe many of her patients were, but I wasn't, and I had trouble with it.

The physical therapist, on the other hand, was great. He gave me a regimen of light stretching exercises which I continue to repeat every morning, even two years later. They help me loosen up and get my blood flowing to start the day.

I start by resting my hands lightly on the back of a chair and doing ten knee bends with my knees directly over my feet. Then I rise onto my toes ten times. I breathe in with the strain and out with the release. Then I walk in place for twenty steps. I kick one foot and then the other to the side twenty times. Then I turn to the side and swing my inside leg forward and back ten times on each side. I move slowly, not sharply, trying not to drag my foot, but to extend it with each backswing.

After that, I sit in a chair and lift both legs for twenty flutter kicks, then lace my fingers behind my head and draw my elbows back five times.

I watched a ballerina do similar exercises at my granddaughter's ballet studio—without the chair. I try to remember that ballerina and keep my movements fluid. Ballerinas are graceful, yet surprisingly strong.

The physical therapist also prescribed a daily walk, which I've been less successful at maintaining but am still working on. I know it's good for me, but it's easy to let it slip from time to time.

Exercise is good for me. Getting out in the fresh air and moving around is good for me. I've started making a point of going places—like the mall or to visit someone in the hospital—where I'll do a lot of walking.

The apostle Paul points out the value of exercise: "For physical training is of some value, but godliness has value for all things, holding promise for both the present and the life to come" (1 Timothy 4:8). Godliness may be more important, but physical training does have value. I need to use my body to be able to get optimum use from it.

According to the Centers for Disease Control and Prevention (CDC), only forty-eight percent of all adults get enough aerobic physical activity to improve their health.[6] Two and a half hours a week of moderate aerobic activity, such as brisk walking, is required. Walking is the most popular physical activity, with about six in ten adults reporting that they walked for at least ten minutes in the previous week.

Physical activity helps control weight and improve health. People who are physically active live longer and have lower risk for heart disease, stroke, type 2 diabetes, depression and some cancers.[7]

With all the emphasis the Bible places on the spiritual, we might conclude that our bodies aren't important, but Paul also writes of the value of our bodies: "Do you not know that your body is a temple of the Holy Spirit, who is in you, whom you have received from God? You are not your own; you were bought at a price. Therefore honor God with your body" (2 Corinthians 6:19-20).

My body is a temple housing God's Spirit of Holiness. I need to take care of it so it will provide as stable a dwelling place as possible.

I've always been somewhat out-of-touch with my body. My interior life has always seemed more important than my external, physical self. But that's a mistake. When I got sick, I couldn't help noticing my body. I felt better about myself as I watched it go from weak to strong, from painful to pleasant, from clumsy to more graceful, from fettered to free. It felt good.

About a year after my surgery, people began telling me how much better I looked than I did when I first got out of the hospital. Even though I felt self-conscious for a while after my surgery, it was important to be around people. At the mall I remember feeling like everybody could see the bumps on my head from the valves there. I also felt hesitant about getting on the escalator. Gradually, I learned to relax and be grateful that I had hair to cover the bumps. Now I walk though the mall and step onto the escalator without fear.

Our minister, Mark Manassee, preached a short sermon series he called "You 2.0," on becoming the best version of ourselves that we can be. That's what I've always wanted to do, and it hasn't changed as I've grown older. As Mark put it, "God is still working on us. We'll never be perfect, but over time, as we open ourselves, we'll be more loving, more forgiving, and have more peace."

Because of what Jesus has done for me, I present myself to Him as a living sacrifice. How I use my body matters. I give my whole self to Him—body, mind, emotions and spirit. Even those parts that let me down, that failed to function as they should. He wants me to give them to Him as an offering, to let Him take them and change them and use them in whatever way pleases Him.

In other words, my exercise, diet, and sleep I get matter. They're all part of the sacrifice I'm giving and being to God.

God can take my weak parts and make them strong. Or He can take my weak parts and use that weakness, as He did with Paul, for His glory (2 Corinthians 12:7-10).

Paul emphasizes the need for discipline in our lives. "Do you not know that in a race all the runners run, but only one gets the prize? Run in such a way as to get the prize. Everyone who competes in the games goes into strict training. They do it to get a crown that will not last; but we do it to get a crown that will last forever. Therefore I do not run like a man running aimlessly; I do not fight like a man beating the air. No, I beat my body and make it my slave so that after I have preached to others, I myself will not be disqualified for the prize" (1 Corinthians 9:24-27).

Discipline, in the abstract, is difficult for me. But once something becomes a habit, it gets a lot easier. I need to turn good health training into a habit. In everything I try to do, from weight reduction to strength training, I need to be in charge, to be making the decisions. I can't let my appetite or my laziness control me.

Exercise isn't just good for my physical body. The increased blood flow from exercise carries needed oxygen to my brain. When I have better circulation, my brain works better, and when I'm in good health generally, I'm less likely to be depressed.

The prize I win isn't a ribbon or a trophy. It's the continued strength and flexibility that allows me to function, the increased blood flow that feeds my body and my brain for maximum efficiency.

Newton's First Law of Motion makes the point. "A body at rest tends to stay at rest, while a body in motion stays in motion." Newton's variable was a force. The body at rest will remain at rest unless acted on by a force. That force has to come from inside me. I can ask Frank to remind me to go for a walk, but he won't always think about it. I need to incorporate it into my daily schedule. No matter how easy it would be to sit in front of the computer or the TV all day, I must move to continue to improve.

And Paul emphasizes obedience. "If anyone competes as an athlete, he does not receive the victor's crown unless he competes according to the rules" (2 Timothy 2:5). God has given us rules that are built into our bodies. If we don't use them, we'll grow weak and incapable.

After just two weeks in the hospital, I was on a walker until I regained my balance and strength. I hated it. It made me self-conscious, and it implied weakness, which wasn't the way I wanted to see myself. I made one week of daily walks around the block with it, and I went to church once with it. By the next week, I was able to give it up. It made me feel good to donate it to someone who needed it, but I was happiest just to be rid of it.

You may not experience the level of healing I did, but you owe it to yourself and to God to do what you can to regain as much strength and mental competence as you can.

Paul also makes the connection between physical and faith training: "I have fought the good fight, I have finished the race, I have kept the faith. Now there is in store for me the crown of righteousness, which the Lord, the righteous judge, will award to me on that day—and not only to me, but also to all who have longed for his appearing" (2 Timothy 4:7-8).

As I draw nearer to the end of my time, I need to continue striving and living faithfully, trusting God for the reward.

Our expert for the Bible class session on physical health was Jeff Nicholson. A physical trainer, Jeff comes from a Vermont family of outdoors people and exercisers. I went to ACC with his mother, June, and stayed with his parents in their home when I spoke for a women's retreat there. Jeff talked with us about maintaining our physical strength and about the sorts of exercises we need to do.

"Our bodies aren't designed to sit," he said. "We're designed to move. The more we use our bodies, the better we function. The worst thing you can do is to sit too long."

He advised us to squat with our heels on the ground and to ask our bodies to do things we have trouble doing: standing from sitting without holding onto something, bending back, lifting an object over our heads, standing with our feet together and reaching back toward our heels.

"Ask your body to do more for strength and flexibility," he said. He recommended strength training with weights, as does the CDC.

But he surprised me by saying that diet is even more important than exercise. We should eat a good variety of natural, not processed, foods. "History is a succession of famine and abundance," he said, "but in our country, we've missed famine, so our problem is that most of us have more fat stored than we need."

A good diet includes plenty of fruit and vegetables (I try for five servings a day), whole grains, lean meat, chicken or fish (a serving is palm-sized) and non-fat dairy products. I prefer a basically Mediterranean diet with olive oil and yogurt, pita bread and hummus — and don't forget the dark chocolate!

The Mayo Clinic's website includes their guidelines for eating with diabetes, which is a great way for all people to eat.[8]

Fortunately, I enjoy good food. I like fruit and vegetables. My biggest problem is taking the time to prepare them. My son, Robert, suggested combining lettuce and fresh spinach in a big bowl to serve up as salads by adding tomatoes and cucumbers one day, and fruit, cheese, and nuts the next.

For Katyana's birthday party, we prepared carrot and celery sticks, and now I'm trying to keep some on hand.

However, the most important thing is not what we eat, but how we eat it. As Paul writes, "So whether you eat or drink or whatever you do, do it all for the glory of God" (1 Corinthians 10:31). We need to eat with gratitude to God for our food, and with prayers for, and creative ways to share with, those who don't have enough.

Contribute to food drives and food banks, and encourage your local congregation to keep food on hand for those who need it. Remember that many people who need food don't have places to prepare it, so in addition to a canned food supply, you'll need to provide smaller bags of ready-to-eat meals that keep well.

"Give us the food we need for each day," I prayed for months after my surgery. We can't pray for bread without thinking about our neighbors who are in need. "Give food to people who are hungry all over the world—in Syria, the Central African Republic, South Sudan, the Philippines, and even here in the U.S."

Many people in the developing world live on $2 or less a day. And two thousand children in Los Angeles County are food deprived. We need to pray: "Help us be moderate in our eating as in all things. And help us trust You to provide what we need, both for ourselves and to be able to share with others." In addition to our regular contribution to the church, we need to contribute to international relief agencies such as Healing Hands International.

Sleep is another component of good physical health. When I go to bed, I check the clock and add eight hours. That gives me the time to wake up. I fall asleep thinking about that time and counting to four, inhaling on "one, two" and exhaling on "three, four." I do it over and over, not thinking of anything else except, perhaps, counting my blessings or praying for people who've requested my prayers or for the needs of people here in L.A. and around the world.

Next thing I know, it's about eight hours later. I've gotten a good night's sleep. I enjoy the way I feel and can perform the next day when I've had enough sleep.

Sleep is a special gift from God. "In vain you rise early and stay up late, toiling for food to eat—for he grants sleep to those he loves" (Psalm 127:2). God gives you sleep. He knows you need it. Relax and rest in Him, and trust Him to give you what you need.

When I first came home from the hospital, I wasn't dreaming. I remember the first night I dreamed. I didn't recall what the dream was about, but the next morning, I knew I had dreamed, and it was the best night's sleep I'd had in a long time. When you're in the hospital, nobody lets you sleep deeply enough to dream. Dreams occur in REM sleep, the deep level of sleep which is most restful.

Like many of you, I get up at least once in the night. That's normal. Generally, I don't turn on lights, but just return to bed and repeat the counting until I drift back off. If I've been sleeping on one side, I try to fall back to sleep on the other.

Our health insurance company, United Healthcare, sends a "Health-e Tool" email each month, and one was on getting a good night's sleep. They suggest having a sleep schedule and a bedtime ritual, not going to bed too hungry or too full, making your bedroom as cool, dark and quiet as possible, limiting daytime naps, and being physically active.

A few other components of physical health include hygiene and caffeine.

I've always been concerned about the pervasiveness of anti-bacterial soap and hand sanitizers. Sure enough, the experts have now determined that too much use can lower one's resistance to germs.

Attitudes have also changed about stimulants such as coffee, tea, or cocoa. Stimulants help burn fat and are a good source of antioxidants. However, they are bad for some conditions, so follow your doctor's advice.

Our bodies are what God has given us to house our brains and our souls. They pump the blood that feeds our brains. We don't want them to wear out before we're through using them. We should nurture and care for them to receive optimum service from them.

As members of our class, we wrote in our journals about our

physical health—what we do to maintain it, and what we can do to improve it so that we can be more like the people God would have us be so we can enjoy our victory lap with strength and energy.

Discussion Questions

1. What do you do to exercise? How can you do more?

2. What can you try to do that is difficult for you?

3. What does your diet look like? How can you improve it?

4. What does it mean to eat a balanced diet? How can you eat food that is better for you?

5. How much sleep do you normally get? How well do you sleep? What could you do to improve your sleep?

6. Do you dream? How important do you think it is to dream? Why?

Bible Study

1. "For _____ _____ is of some value, but _____ has value for all things, holding the promise for both the present and the life to come" (1 Timothy 4:8).

2. "Do you not know that in a race all the runners run, but only one gets the prize? Run in such a way as to get the prize. Everyone who competes in the games goes into _____ _____. They do it to get a crown that will not last; but we do it to get a crown that will last forever. Therefore I do not run like

a man running aimlessly; I do not fight like a man beating the air. No, I beat my _____ and make it my _____ so that after I have preached to others, I myself will not be disqualified for the prize" (1 Corinthians 9:24-27).

3. "If anyone competes as an _____, he does not receive the victor's _____ unless he competes according to the _____ " (2 Timothy 2:5).

4. "I have fought the good _____, I have finished the _____, I have kept the faith. Now there is in store for me the _____ of righteousness, which the Lord, the righteous judge, will award me on that day — and not only for me but also to all who have _____ for his appearing" (2 Timothy 4:6-8).

5. "So whether you _____ or _____ or whatever you do, do it all for the _____ of God" (1 Corinthians 10:31).

6. "In vain you rise _____ and stay up _____, toiling for food to eat — for he grants _____ to those he loves: (Psalm 127:2).

Write in Your Journal

Write in your journal about your physical health and what you do to maintain it. What could you do to be more like the person God would have you be physically?

Endnotes

6 http://www.cdc.gov/physicalactivity/data/facts.html.

7 http://americannewsreport.com/more-americans-are-walking-but-they-need-to-pick-up-the-pace-8815304.

8 http://www.mayoclinic.org/diseases-conditions/diabetes/in-depth/diabetes-diet/art-20044295

CHAPTER 4

How Can We Maintain
Our Mental Health?

One Sunday morning when my daughter, Kathy, picked me up for church, I left my purse at home. I felt more than a little undone all morning. I had to remind myself that forgetting my purse wasn't something that couldn't be remedied. Without my checkbook, I couldn't write my usual contribution check, but I could double my contribution the next week. Without my glasses, I couldn't follow the reading, so I just listened, probably more attentively than usual. Without pen and paper for taking notes, I listened to the lesson as well, carrying on an active call-and-response with the minister in my mind.

I could sing. I could pray. I could welcome visitors and hug a friend who was going into the hospital the following week for cancer surgery. I did all that, and I started to feel better about myself.

I have to watch myself when things like that happen. Since the surgery, it's easy to see every mental slip-up as a catastrophe. I haven't just walked off without my purse—something anybody can do. My temptation is to feel that I'm on the verge of dementia.

When I had brain surgery followed by a seizure and a case of pneumonia, I thought my life was over. In the past, for a person my age, any of the three could, and probably would, have been lethal. But today, we're surviving physical challenges that killed people generations earlier. Thus, most of us probably are more concerned about maintaining our mental health and acuity.

The World Health Organization defines health as "a state of complete physical, mental, and social well-being and not merely the absence of disease or infirmity. Because mental health is essential to overall health and well-being, it must be recognized and treated in all Americans, including older adults, with the same urgency as physical health."[9]

"Most older adults are experiencing the life satisfaction, social and emotional support, and good mental health that are essential to healthy aging," according to a brief on "The State of Mental Health and Aging in America," released by the CDC.[10]

"Some twenty percent of people age fifty-five and older experience some type of mental health concern," according to the American Association of Geriatric Psychiatry. The most common conditions include anxiety, severe cognitive impairment, and mood disorders (such as depression or bipolar disorder).[11]

Depression is not a normal part of growing older, and in eighty percent of cases, it is treatable. In my case, it has occurred twice: the result of the failure of an effort I had poured my life into, and the result of a serious illness. In both cases, it improved when I recognized the problem, talked about it, and sought and received counseling or medical help.

The first instance was in 2003, when Life Skills Lab failed after I had put so much time and effort into building it. My mother invited me to come to Lubbock, Texas, to visit her. Her friend, Carolyn Rhodes, an excellent Bible teacher, came over to talk and pray with me.

Carolyn recommended that I read and pray and meditate on 2 Timothy 1:7. It was the first time I'd paid close attention to the verse. In the King James Version, it reads: "For God did not give us a spirit of fear, but a spirit of power, of love and of a sound mind."

As I meditated on that scripture, I realized that my depression had its roots in fear. I had stepped out in faith to do a big job, and at first, God seemed to have been with me, guiding and strengthening me. But then things began to go wrong. Enrollment grew from six to about a dozen students, but we never had the numbers our board anticipated. Support from members of my congregation was outstanding. We had approximately fifty volunteers for each of the three classes each year, but we never had the continuing stream of funding we needed to sustain the program financially.

I was tired, sick, and discouraged. Had God forsaken me? Had my faith failed? Faith is the opposite of fear. "Fear not," is a message that runs throughout the Bible. God wanted me to have power, love and a sound mind. Power was all but inconceivable at that point.

I felt loved by my family and friends who were trying to help me through that rough patch. But a sound mind seemed to be basic and was the theme of most of my prayers at that time.

It came back to me after my illness and again became the theme of my prayers.

Because I write my prayers in my journal, I can track my recovery as I read through it: "Grant me greater coordination and a greater ability to think things through." "Grant me strength and a sound mind." "Help me grow more competent in everything from writing to housework. Help me get things done better." "Thank You that I've been improving regularly. I don't know how total my recovery will be, but I know I'm in Your hands, and that's a safe place to be." "Thank You that I'm coming out of my dark night of the soul. Thank You for Your light, which is lighting my path. May it light the paths of all who reach out to You."

These are the things we can pray about and try to maintain, but some things are beyond our powers. We may need to seek professional help. When I began having physical and mental trouble in Spring 2012, I went to our family doctor, who sent me to a neurologist. She had me take a series of tests, including an MRI, which revealed that my brain was producing too much fluid on the right side. It was interfering with both my physical and my mental balance.

She also had me take a battery of neuropsychiatric tests and perform a series of physical activities in her office to indicate how well my brain was controlling my body.

She sent me to a neurosurgeon who placed a shunt in my head to drain the fluid. I've always enjoyed reading and writing, teaching and learning. But when I had brain surgery, I wondered if

I would ever be able to do those things again.

Eventually, I was able to give away my walker, continue my website, read about thirty books in the latter half of the year, and solve crossword puzzles. My faith and strength were returning as my brain began to function better. The love of my family, church family, friends, and neighbors contributed greatly to my healing.

Follow-up MRIs and neuropsychiatric tests were administered nearly two years later. The MRI showed "stable appearance of the ventricular catheter and ventricular configuration. There is no hydrocephalus," and the neuropsychiatric tests indicated "improved performance on virtually all measures of information processing and psychomotor speed."

I was encouraged to use checklists, planners, and calendars, which I'd done for years, and to "continue to stay active and engaged in stimulating activities," which I was eager to do.

An article by Margery D. Rosen, in the April 2014 edition of the *AARP Bulletin*, quotes P. Murali Doraiswamy, M.D. and co-author of *The Alzheimer's Action Plan:* "You should know that more than 100 disorders—from the side effects of medication to urinary tract infections—can also trigger dementia-like symptoms. Some of these conditions are not serious, but they're often missed or misdiagnosed in seniors."

The article lists eight common disorders that mimic dementia, starting with the one I had: normal pressure hydrocephalus. Other potential problems include drug interactions, depression, urinary tract infection, thyroid, vitamin B-12 deficiency, diabetes, and alcohol abuse. If you're afraid you might be suffering from dementia, have a doctor check first for one of these other causes of your symptoms. Most are easily treatable.

If you're taking prescriptions for several different physical difficulties, consider having a single doctor review everything you're taking to assure that your medicines aren't reacting with one another. That has happened with people I've known, and when the real chemical reaction is addressed, I've seen them experience an amazing recovery.

This is good news. It may not be as bad as we think. We shouldn't jump to conclusions.

Unfortunately, depressive disorders are widely under-recognized and often go untreated among older adults. Still, nearly ninety percent of adults age 50 or older indicated that they are receiving adequate amounts of support.[12]

Nearly ninety-five percent of adults 50 and older report being "satisfied" or "very satisfied" with their lives. Surprisingly, adults age 50-64 were more likely than adults 65 or older to report dissatisfaction with their lives. In 2006, the prevalence of frequent mental distress was 9.2% among adults 50 and older and only 6.5% among those over 65.[13]

That may have to do with the fact that younger old people are still persisting in unrealistic expectations, while the older olds are making peace with aging.

None of us has a perfect life, but for those who expect to, old age will be a disappointment. I'll never be as successful, as beautiful, as popular, or as respected as I always hoped I'd be. I'll never write the Great American Novel or win a Pulitzer or found a major nonprofit that outlives me. I began to realize that before I turned 65, and I've made peace with it since I turned 70. The best I can hope for is to do my best at whatever age.

Many of the principles about exercising our bodies to help maintain physical health apply to our mental health as well. It's important to exercise our brains. We do that by reading, writing, working puzzles of various sorts, and maintaining an interest in, and interaction with, the world around us. Even physical exercise makes our blood flow faster and helps our brains as well, by carrying more oxygen to them. If we're still having problems, we need to recognize that fact, go to the doctor to find out what's wrong, and follow his or her instructions.

In my case, my regular doctor referred me to a neurologist who, after a series of tests, referred me to other specialists.

We think of our minds in two basic senses. There's the physical brain that is an organ in our bodies, and there's the consciousness, with its jumble of thoughts from the mundane to the sublime. A sound mind involves both senses of the word. The physical brain itself needs to be sound, as do the thoughts coming from it.

Scripture, for the most part, deals with the latter. God cares a lot more about *what* we think than *how well* we do it. "We have the mind of Christ," we're told (1 Corinthians 2:16). The mind of Christ means the attitude Jesus showed when He lived on earth as a person.

Paul, in his letter to the church at Philippi, writes, "Your attitude should be the same as that of Christ Jesus: who, being in the very nature God, did not consider equality with God something to be grasped, but made himself nothing, taking the very nature of a servant, being made in human likeness. And, being found in appearance as a man, he humbled himself and became obedient to death—even death on a cross!" (Philippians 2:5-8).

We often consider how we can rise in the world, but, as usual, Jesus turned everything upside down. For Him, the way up was down—not pride, but humility, not leadership but servanthood, not running things but being obedient until death.

Paul continues in Philippians 4 to give us more direct instructions about our attitude: "Rejoice in the Lord always. I will say it again: Rejoice! Let your gentleness be evident to all. The Lord is near. Do not be anxious about anything but in everything, by prayer and petition, with thanksgiving, present your requests to God. And the peace of God, which transcends all understanding, will guard your hearts and your minds in Christ Jesus." (Philippians 4:4-7).

What are some of the thoughts that keep us from rejoicing? They include grudges, perceived slights, and biases fed by negative media. If the media you watch feeds your anger, hatred, or other negative emotions, change channels.

People may try to tell you that attitudes can't be commanded, but to me, Paul seems to be commanding us to be happy, just as surely as Peter commanded his listeners on the day of Pentecost to repent and be baptized. And if he commanded it, we can do it.

We can look for the good in everything that happens. We can see God behind the events of our lives. And we can do what we can to bring about the good we're seeking. Scientists have just begun talking about the positive effect a good attitude has on the brain. When we are happy, confident, and grateful, our minds are less troubled.

Paul goes on to talk even about the specific content of our thoughts: "Whatever is true, whatever is noble, whatever is right, whatever is pure, whatever is lovely, whatever is admirable—if anything is excellent or praiseworthy—think about such things." (Philippians 4:8).

Anxiety is among the most prevalent mental health problems among older adults. We are anxious about our health, about our families, about crime, about politics. However, more than ninety percent of adults 50 and older did not report a lifetime diagnosis of anxiety, with only 12.7% among adults age 50-64 and 7.6% among those over 65 doing so.[14] In other words, for most of us, anxiety is more a matter of negative content we take into our brains, not an actual mental illness.

To avoid anxiety, we need to avoid holding grudges and learn to forgive. We need to avoid perceived slights, negative commentary, and bias—looking for good in the things we listen to and the people around us. If we find ourselves giving in to the negative, we should re-evaluate our thinking and seek to be kinder, more accepting people.

One member of our church family, Dwayne Simmons, teaches neurophysics at UCLA. Dwayne was able to reassure me throughout the process that the medical procedure I was to undergo wasn't as bad as it sounded. He also was the expert who spoke with our class about the latest discoveries in brain science, one of the fastest-growing areas of medical research.

Dwayne speaks often on the relationship between Christianity and science. He was also involved in President Obama's initiative for brain research. When he visited our class, he handed out diagrams of the brain, showing how a healthy brain processes information:[15]

First, my eyes see something and transmit the image along the optic nerve.

Second, my visual cortex at the back of my brain identifies what my eyes have seen.

Third, association areas throughout my brain determine whether the scene is important and how it relates to me.

Fourth, the hippocampus, a hook-shaped area in the middle of the brain, encodes what I see into memory.

Finally, the prefrontal cortex determines what I should do about it. The most complex reasoning and planning occurs here as the axons, the transmission lines that carry information, branch out at their ends into synapses.

Synapses are tiny bridges that allow neurons to communicate with one another. Dwayne gave us the great news that our brains continue to produce these vital synapses throughout our lives.

We can continue learning all our lives.

This is good news for all of us. It means that we're living at a great time to maintain a "sound mind."

The handout also suggested five ways to slow the effects of aging on our brains:

1. Calm Down. Stress can destroy synapses.

2. Exercise. The increased blood flow to the brain during and after a workout may help keep synapses strong.

3. Make Friends. Social interaction boosts brain function, possibly because it requires effort from many areas. Too many people — even Christians — appreciate Jesus but have problems with people. However, the people around us are among our greatest gifts from God. The people in our families, our churches, our neighborhoods, our work, and social lives give us a built-in group of people with similar beliefs and goals with whom we can share our interests and concerns at any stage of our lives.

4. Do What You Do Best. Expertise remains intact throughout life. I may forget where I left my glasses, but I can write.

5. Sleep Well. Inferior sleep can impair the ability to learn. According to research at the University of Massachusetts, fragmented sleep robs the brain of time in the sleep stages that are critical to processing information. I had been correct when I identified a good night's sleep and dreams as part of my healing.

How can you maintain your mental health? Exercise your brain by reading, writing, and solving problems and puzzles.

Supplement your brain by planning, writing notes, and keeping a calendar.

Have your doctors check you for diseases that mimic dementia.

Have a single doctor check your prescriptions to avoid drug interactions.

Monitor your thoughts to see that they're positive and Christ-like. Look for the good in all the circumstances of your lives. Relax, exercise, make friends, keep doing the things you do well, and get plenty of sleep.

I can't tell you what a thrill it was to put together and teach the Bible class upon which this book was based. For over a year, I had been thinking about these topics and what they meant for me. I know that many people do. That's why I was eager to get a group together to share our ideas and concerns about aging, and what has proved effective for each of us.

The class talked about our own brain health. We wrote in our journals about our faith in God. How did we come to it? How do we sustain it? What do we do to exercise and stimulate our brains? Do we concentrate on others and their needs? Are our thoughts primarily positive?

As we proceed on the victory lap of our lives, we will experience some loss in mental powers, just as we do in the physical. But there are plenty of things we can do to prolong brain health and live happy, productive lives. Now where did I put my glasses?

Discussion Questions

1. What do you do to exercise your brain? What can you add that might help?

2. What do you do physically that can keep that blood flowing to your brain as well as your other organs? What can you add that might help?

3. What is the connection between faith and fear?

4. What can you do to increase your faith and decrease your fear?

5. How can you nourish your social contacts?

6. How can you find ways to continue doing what you do best? What did you do well in school or on the job?

Bible Study

1. "For God did not give us a spirit of _____, but a spirit of

   _____, of _____ and of a _____

   _____" (2 Timothy 1:7, KJV)

2. "We have the_____ of _____"

   (1 Corinthians 2:16).

3. "Your _____ should be the same

   as that of _____ _____: who, being

   in the very _____ God, did not consider

   equality with God something to be grasped, but made himself nothing,

   taking the very nature of a _____,

   being made in human likeness. And, being found in appearance as

   a man, he _____himself and became

_____ to death — even death on a cross!" (Philippians 2:5-8).

4. "_____ in the Lord always. I will say it again: _____! Let your _____ _____ be evident to all. The Lord is near. Do not be _____ about anything but in everything, by prayer and petition, with _____, present your requests to God. And the peace of God, which transcends all understanding, will guard your hearts and your _____ in Christ Jesus." (Philippians 4:4-7).

5. "Whatever is _____, whatever is _____, whatever is _____, whatever is _____, whatever is _____, whatever is _____ — if anything is _____ or _____ — think about such things." (Philippians 4:8).

Write in Your Journal

Write in your journal about your faith in God. How did you come to it? How do you sustain it? What can you do to exercise your brain? How can you get more physical exercise and improve the flow of blood to your brain?

Endnotes

9 http://www.cdc.gov/aging/pdf/mental_health.pdf.

10 Ibid.

11 Ibid.

12 http://www.cdc.gov/aging/pdf/mental_health.pdf.

13 Ibid.

14 http://www.cdc.gov/aging/pdf/mental_health.pdf.

15 http://media-cache-cd0.pinimg.com/736x/c9/c4/c6/
c9c4c6d568d05d281364f5c6a2e072d4.jpg.

CHAPTER 5

How Can We Maintain
Our Emotional Health?

One of my happiest recent memories is the celebration of mine and Frank's 50th wedding anniversary in August 2013. About twenty members of his choral music singing group, Mansfield Chamber Singers, joined some sixty members of our church, and twenty special guests from various periods of our lives together for a salad luncheon that included tribute speeches and a singalong of 60s folk music and protest songs.

By the end, we were all singing, clapping, and rejoicing together as we celebrated love and peace, freedom and brotherhood.

Ken Wells, the director of the Mansfield group, talked about Frank and our connection with the songs they were performing. One of our elders, Keith Brisco, compared our marriage to a movie with a script and a soundtrack (referring to my writing and Frank's music), and our son, Robert, told about the "good rules" he had observed that made our marriage work — mutual support, communication (including listening), respect and love.

A friend from church, Troy Pearson, took photos, and Kathy put seven of them onto a mousepad that sits beside my computer keyboard. Every morning, when I get up to start working on my website or other writings, I see pictures of my high school friend, Bonnie Leicht, who came from Texas to celebrate with us; of our friends from the Vermont Avenue church, Joe and Betty Bridges, who celebrated their 50th anniversary the same year; of our family singing with the Mansfield Chamber Singers; and a close-up that I particularly love of Frank's hand holding mine on the corner of the table. It starts my day with a smile.

Kathy also created a lovely book of photos of us through the years. It had spaces for those attending to write their comments. I love to pick it up and read through the messages.

She also made us a scrapbook from photos of the event. Ron Cox, our associate minister, took a video. They bring tears to my eyes and a smile to my lips when I look at them. They are tears of joy and gratitude — to everyone who attended and took part and sent presents, cards and emails. I also have immense gratitude to Frank for putting up with a lifetime of me and to God for helping me find the only man who could have put up with me that long.

Do we grow more emotional as we grow older? I think I do. I find myself tearing up more often at everything from movies, to books and memories to the news. I laugh more easily, too, at jokes and just the funny things that happen in everyday life. I feel closer to Frank, our children, Katyana. I want to demonstrate my love more freely with hugs, kisses, and cuddles for my family and friends.

Maybe that's all it is. Maybe I've just stopped being embarrassed by my emotions. I feel freer to show what I feel. That's probably a good thing.

What are the primary emotions I feel as I grow older?

I feel *love*—a tremendous outpouring of love for my family, friends, and church family.

I feel *anxiety*. I'm stepping out into unknown territory. I've never been this old before, this near to death, this aware of the uncertainty of life, of my lack of control over what happens.

I feel *fear*—at least at night when I'm at home alone, when I go to confront a neighbor about playing his music so loudly that it drowns out the TV in the room with me, when the police caught the man in the apartment a block from our house who had made 17 pipe bombs.

I feel *joy*—a deep, profound joy as I look back over my life. The challenge of work, the delight of discovery, the wonder of child-birth, the pleasure of traveling, the satisfaction of ministry, the thrill of praising God in song, and the pure elation of having spent half a century with the man I love have all been joyous events.

According to a recent Stanford study published in the journal *Psychology and Aging*, we tend to become more emotionally stable as we grow older. That translates into longer, more productive lives that offer more benefits than problems, according to the study's lead author, Laura Carstensen.[16]

"As people age, they're more emotionally balanced and better able to solve highly emotional problems," she said. "We may be seeing a larger group of people who can get along with a greater number of people. They care more and are more compassionate about problems, and that may lead to a more stable world."

Compassion is the emotion with which I most want to be identified with. Jesus was known for His compassion. The word appears ten times in the Gospels to describe Him. A common phrase is, "Jesus, moved with compassion...."

He didn't just feel things; He was motivated by His feelings to help.

Compassion is a combination of the prefix *com-*, meaning *with*, and *passion, feeling*. It means to feel with, share the feelings of someone else, know what it's like.

Like Jesus, I'd like not just to understand what it feels like (to be poor, to be discriminated against, to be oppressed) but to do something to make things better.

"As people get older, they're more aware of mortality," Carstensen said. "So when they see or experience moments of wonderful things, that often comes with the realization that life is fragile and will come to an end. But that's a good thing. It's a signal of strong emotional health and balance." She attributes the change to her theory of "socio-emotional selectivity," people investing in what's most important to them when time is limited.

I've always been keenly aware of time and of the importance of using it well. I even wrote a book with Helen Young called *Time Management for Christian Women*. But only recently have I been so aware of time running out. And, what hardly seems fair, of its passing even faster as it runs out!

Positive thinking and action may improve my physical health as well as my mind. My insurance company, United Healthcare, offered what they called a "Happiness Guide" kit,[17] a guide to practicing positivity, which might help improve your health.

It encourages us to do the following:

1. **Appreciate** — Spend 15 minutes before you go to bed at night jotting down something for which you're grateful and sending a postcard to thank someone for being a part of your life.

2. **Move** — Walk five days a week. Say hello to neighbors, visit, breathe deeply, and take in the beauty around you. Teach someone young an old dance. Exercise your mind by tackling a brain teaser or crossword puzzle.

3. **Smile** — Watch a funny movie or pet video. A good laugh can reduce blood pressure and stress, improve alertness and memory. Put a positive spin on things. Optimism has been linked to a healthy immune system.

4. **Love** — Visit an animal shelter and pet the animals if it's OK with the shelter. Start a garden or grow indoor plants. Spend an afternoon sharing memories with friends. Take photos with you if you have them. Show how much a loved one or friend means to you with a simple hug, kiss, high-five or pat on the back.

5. **Connect** — Visit your local coffee shop and get to know the regulars and staff. Join a club [or church] and get involved

at least four times a month. Work with others toward a common goal. Visit with neighbors. Call your grandkids. Email a friend. Send cards and letters to people.

6. **Give** — Create a "giving fund." Save a little each month, then give it to a favorite charity at the end of the year. Those of us who are Christians already have a giving plan, but we should always be open to ways to expand it. Volunteer. Not only do you help others, but you gain opportunities to learn and socialize. Leave a legacy. It can be monetary or it can be stories from your childhood or special mementos to hand down.

7. **Reflect** — List several positive things you've accomplished in life. Read the list daily. Look in a mirror and say something you like about yourself. Start a positivity diary and write down positive thoughts and happenings each day. Save your notes to re-read next year.

8. **Enjoy** — Every meal offers a chance to slow down and enjoy delicious food. Practice deep breathing to reduce anxiety, lower blood pressure, and feel more energetic. Add the colors you love to your life. If you can't paint an entire room, decorate with flowers or candles. Or add a new shirt in your favorite color to your wardrobe.

9. **Share** — Buy someone coffee, give a compliment, discuss a good book, send a get-well card, laugh, spend time with a grandchild, or let someone in line ahead of you.

The kit from the insurance company includes a notepad for making the suggested lists, as well as postcards to send to friends.

It's not enough just to think positive thoughts and do positive deeds. You also need to address your negative emotions by turning them over to God in prayer. Peter writes, "Cast all your anxiety on him because he cares for you" (1 Peter 5:7).

What steps can you take to control your emotions? How can you avoid getting bogged down in negative emotions? How can you give more control to God? In your journal, write about how you can encourage positive emotions. Write about negative emotions you can allow to rule your thinking. List three steps you plan to take to give God control of these negative emotions.

What is the role of music in lifting your spirits? When I was a child, our family sang together in the car and as we worked at night on the newspaper. I still enjoy listening to music or singing in church or in the shower. My husband, Frank, rehearses every week with his singing group for the concerts they perform twice a year. Singing lifts his spirit, and the rehearsals give him the opportunity to spend time with friends he's known for decades.

Therapy can help. Michael Kirby Smith wrote in *The New York Times* about an 86-year-old man who struggled with "the demise of a long-term business partnership and the sudden death of his first wife eighteen years ago. He worried about his children and grandchildren, and his current wife, Carole."[18]

"When I hit my 80s I thought,... 'I don't know how long I'm going to live. I want to make it easier.'" He began seeing a therapist once a month, exploring the problems that were weighing on him.

Seniors generally have a higher satisfaction rate in therapy than younger people because they're more serious about it. "Older patients realize that time is limited and precious and not to be wasted," says Dr. Robert C. Abrams, professor of clinical psychiatry at Weill Cornell Medical College in Manhattan. "They tend to be serious about the discussion and less tolerant of wasted time. They make great patients."[19]

More than 6.5 million Americans over age 65 suffer from depression, according to the National Alliance on Mental Illness. Although some people our age grew up equating depression with mental illness, that is not always the case. Though some older people may be grappling with unaddressed mental health issues, most are just concerned about living arrangements, finances, chronic health problems, the loss of loved ones, and their own mortality.

That's my problem. Having lived with my own consciousness for 70 years, it's difficult to imagine a world without me. Death is the great unknown. It's a serious concern, and it's worth giving thought to how I can best spend the time I have left.

"In the past, the assumption was that if older people were acting strangely or having problems, it was probably dementia. But now the awareness of depression, anxiety disorders and substance abuse as possible problems has grown," according to Bob G. Knight, professor of gerontology and psychology at the

University of Southern California and author of "Psychotherapy with Older Adults."[20]

Jenny Ricker, a psychologist, met with our Bible class on aging. She suggested keeping a gratitude journal. She talked about Todd Snelgrove, who in his later years spent time at a local restaurant, where he developed strong social ties that brought joy to his life. She talked about the importance of touch, through either hugs and pets, for older people. She talked about depression, grief, and loss, calling our culture "a culture of denial." She recommended affirmations and keeping journals.

Scripture tells us, "You... are controlled not by the sinful nature but by the Spirit, if the Spirit of God lives in you. And if anyone does not have the Spirit of Christ, he does not belong to Christ. But if Christ is in you, your body is dead because of sin, yet your spirit is alive because of righteousness. And if the Spirit of him who raised Jesus from the dead is living in you, he who raised Christ from the dead will also give life to your mortal bodies through his Spirit, who lives in you" (Romans 8:9-11).

God's Spirit lives in all of us who have come into relationship with Christ. And God's Spirit makes us alive. That doesn't just—right this minute, in this life. God's Spirit, the Holy Spirit, the Spirit of Holiness is life-giving. He has promised to live in us when we put on Christ, and if you are living in Jesus, the Holy Spirit is living in you. The Spirit gives life—joyous, affirming, jubilant life.

Paul, in his letter to the Galatian church, tells us, "I have been crucified with Christ and I no longer live, but Christ lives in me. The life I live in the body I live by faith in the Son of God, who loved me and gave himself for me" (Galatians 2:20). This means that, if we're living in Christ, we have faith—his faith. And perfect faith casts out fear.

He also points out that "the fruit of the Spirit is love, joy, peace, patience, kindness, goodness, faithfulness, gentleness and self-control. Against such things there is no law" (Galatians 5: 22-23). When we're in Christ, the Holy Spirit living in us is like a tree heavy with the fruit of emotional health and well-being.

In his letter to the church at Philippi, Paul says, "and this is my prayer: that your love may abound more and more in knowledge and depth of insight, so that you may be able to discern what is best and may be pure and blameless until the day of Christ, filled with the fruit of righteousness that comes through Jesus Christ—to the glory and praise of God" (Philippians 1:9-11).

It always surprises me to read someone writing about Christianity as a joyless, bleak, or solemn religion. It's just the opposite. It's full of joy. And Christian people have every reason to be joyful. Continuing in the book of Philippians, Paul writes: "I am not saying this because I am in need, for I have learned to be content whatever the circumstances. I know what it is to be in need, and I know what it is to have plenty. I have learned the secret of being content in any and every situation, whether well fed or hungry, whether living in plenty or in want. I can do everything through him who gives me strength" (Philippians 4:11-13).

The U.S. is wonderful in many ways, but one of the ways it isn't so great is the attitude it encourages about physical things. Our culture doesn't encourage us to be content with what we have. And yet, Christianity, which most people consider a large part of our culture, not merely encourages but even commands us to be content.

Our culture seems to bend over backward to make us feel *discontented* with our material belongings. And yet, our houses are full of things. We don't have room in our garage for our car because it's so full of things. And a whole new industry has arisen to store the overflow in individual, climate-controlled units.

As Nancy Twigg wrote in *From Clutter to Clarity*:[21]

If your contentment depends on your circumstances, you'll never be truly content because life's circumstances will never be completely perfect. True contentment is not having everything you want, but learning to appreciate everything you have .... Contentment is being able to come to terms with where you are and what's going on in your life, even if it's not what you would have chosen for yourself.

We may discover that what we'd planned for ourselves isn't nearly so wonderful as what God has planned for us.

Jesus told the soldiers who came to Him asking what they should do to "be content with your pay" (Luke 3:14). How many of us who are working are satisfied with our pay? Whatever we're making, we think it should be more. That's not God's way. That's the way of the world—materialistic, ambitious, and proud.

Paul warns his young minister friend to resist the tendency to want more: "But godliness with contentment is great gain. For we brought nothing into the world, and we can take nothing out of it. But if we have food and clothing, we will be content with that. People who want to get rich fall into temptation and a trap and into many foolish and harmful desires that plunge men [and women] into ruin and destruction. For the love of money is a root of all kinds of evil. Some people, eager for money, have wandered from the faith and pierced themselves with many griefs" (1 Timothy 6:6-10). As we grow older, we should learn to live and to value living more simply.

The writer to the Hebrews says, "Keep your lives free from the love of money and be content with what you have" (Hebrews 13:5).

Contentment may not sound like a sexy emotion, but it is perhaps the most important element in a life that ends well. If you can be content with what you have, with the wonderful blessings God has given you, you'll have been successful in growing old.

I've been working on contentment most of my life. I am writing this from the perspective of someone who has never been rich—probably never even been what you'd call middle class. As a child in my parents' home, we worked hard just to put food on the table. And, if my grandfather hadn't owned a dry goods store, I don't know what we would have done for clothes—or a house, for that matter.

As our family was growing up, Frank and I never had much. We both worked, but this is Los Angeles, and everything costs more. We never owned our own home until the kids were grown. We were able to buy into the housing market mostly because of the legacy my mother left me when she died. We are happy to have a place where we can live, where family and friends can gather, and where we can live out our lives with the assurance that some landlord can't decide they need us to move out so they can move *their* children in, especially since that actually happened to us more than once when we were renting.

We have food, clothing, and shelter, and we are content. We have friends and we have each other. We have feelings that we're comfortable expressing. We have compassion, and we act on that compassion as we're able. And we are content. Contentment goes a long way toward making the end of life a true victory lap.

Discussion Questions

1. What steps can we take to control our emotions?

2. How can we give more of the control to God?

3. What is the role of gratitude in our emotional health?

4. What is the relationship between our social lives and our emotional health?

5. Discuss the role of music in maintaining your contentment.

6. How can we be more content?

Bible Study

1. "If Christ is in you, your body is dead because of sin, yet your
   _____ is alive because of righteousness. And if the
   _____ of him who raised Jesus from the dead
   is living in you, he who raised Christ from the dead will also give
   _____ to your mortal bodies through the
   _____, who lives in you" (Romans 8:10-11).

2. "I have been _____ with _____
   and I no longer live, but Christ _____ in me. The life I
   live in the body I live by _____ in the Son of God, who
   _____ me and gave himself for me"
   (Galatians 2:20).

3. "The fruit of the Spirit is _____,
   _____, _____, _____,
   _____, _____,
   _____and _____
   _____"(Galatians 5:22-23).

4. "I have learned to be _____ whatever the
   _____" (Philippians 4:11).

5. "Be content with your _____" (Luke 3:14).

6. "Keep your lives free from the _____ of _____,
   and be _____with what you have" (Hebrews 13:5).

Write in Your Journal

Write about negative emotions you allow to rule your thinking. List three steps you plan to give God greater control.

Endnotes

16 http://news.stanford.edu/news/2010/october/older-happy-study-102710.html.

17 https://www.uhcmedicaresolutions.com/pdf/ma_svn/UHC_Renew_Newsletter_Issue2_MA_MAPD.pdf.

18 http://well.blogs.nytimes.com/2013/04/22/how-therapy-can-help-in-the-golden-years/?_php=true&_type=blogs&_r=0.

19 Ibid.

20 Ibid.

CHAPTER 6

How Can We Maintain Our Spiritual Health?

Most mornings, I get up and write in my journal. I've kept journals for decades. It was important while I was working to orient myself to the new day and its demands. It's still important today to ensure that I'm putting the time I have left to good use.

I date the page, check the weather forecast, and write a sentence about what the day is going to be like. That helps me select appropriate clothes to wear. Then I look back over the previous day and list what I did. A typical day might include a card or letter to a friend, a chapter on a book or working on my website, and cleaning a room or organizing files or a drawer or cabinet.

Next, I look ahead to the new day and plan the activities I'd like to accomplish. I end by writing a prayer, thanking God for His many blessings and seeking His guidance in my work and His help for me and for others who need it. In addition to the sick, the bereaved, the unemployed and the homeless, I pray for the hungry, those who lack access to clean drinking water or other necessities, victims of war and of natural disasters around the world.

I don't worry if I miss a day—or even a week, as I did when I had surgery. It's better to write as often as possible than to worry about keeping a complete record.

Some years ago, I taught an adult Bible class on journaling. I called it "Journaling Through the Bible: a Voyage of Self-Discovery and Bible Learning." It included different approaches to journaling: discovery, truth, meditation, celebration, growth, exploration, observation, visualization, dreams, love, dialogue, dedication, and creativity. I encouraged the class members to stretch themselves as they journal. Currently, I'm teaching a similar class to a group of teenagers.

I've always been attracted to the things of the spirit. Jimmy Townsend stated it well, as quoted in Jimmy Carter's *Virtues of Aging*, "We worry too much about something to live on—and too little about something to live for."[22]

As a lifelong Christian who attended worship and Bible classes as a child, was baptized at 13, attended Christian colleges where I took Bible classes, and, as an adult, has taught classes, written, and spoken widely on Christianity, and has journaled for more than thirty years, I never expected to have problems with my spiritual health. But that struck me as well when I fell ill.

God has always seemed close. I've journaled, prayed, meditated, and studied. I've had a rich spiritual life. But with physical, mental, and emotional frailty, my spiritual health suffered, too.

Just when I needed God the most, my faith in God and His love and care weakened. I experienced a desert of the soul, a bleak depression.

Despite the fact that I've discussed physical, mental and emotional health as separate aspects in this book, they're so intertwined that a difficulty in one area can't help but affect the rest, just as stubbing your toe or striking your elbow can reverberate through your whole body.

I needed to improve physically, mentally, and emotionally to renew my spiritual health. And I needed to recover my spiritual health to improve otherwise.

Spiritual health is more than just a warm feeling. It's about relationships with God, Christ, and the Holy Spirit. It's also about our relationships with God's people, the church, as well as with the world around us.

According to the Merck Manual for Health Care Professionals, some ninety percent of elderly people consider themselves both religious and spiritual. "For most of the elderly in the U.S., religion has a major role in their life. Ninety-six percent believe in God or a universal spirit. Ninety percent pray. And fifty percent attend religious services weekly or more often. The level of religious participation among the elderly is greater than that of any other age group.[23]

"Religion correlates with improved physical and mental health. However, experts cannot determine whether religion contributes to health or whether psychologically or physically healthier people are attracted to religious groups," the Merck writer says.

Benefits listed include:

- A positive and hopeful attitude about life and illness, which predicts improved health outcomes and lower mortality rates

- A sense of meaning and purpose in life, which affects health behaviors and social and family relationships

- A greater ability to cope with illness and disability

What do you do to maintain spiritual health? How can you grow closer to God? How can you grow closer to His church and how can you grow closer to the world around you?

Again, it involves exercise. We exercise our spiritual muscles by spending time with God—in public worship and private devotions, by listening to and meditating on His Word, and by singing His praises.

We grow closer to His church by spending time with His people—talking deeply with them, getting to know their challenges and needs, interceding for them with our Heavenly Father and theirs, and doing acts of kindness for one another and together for those outside the faith who have needs.

And we grow closer to the world around us by getting involved with our neighbors and our community, by keeping up with news, and by volunteering with the church or a local school or nonprofit to help some group we're concerned about—the homeless, children, teens, widows, the needy. We also grow closer to the world by praying for its needs.

We need to be consistent. The way we live should show how

important these relationships are to us. Taking our eyes off ourselves and putting them on God and on other people can help us maintain our mental and emotional health as well.

That was my biggest problem. I was so concerned about myself that I allowed myself to be distracted from God.

It didn't happen when I was in the hospital. There, I was looking for God's hand, and I saw it everywhere—in the kindness of the nurses, the efficiency of the doctors, the concern expressed by everyone that I understand what they were doing and why. I saw it in the young Mexican man who talked to me about angels, in the young African-American vocational nurse who braided my hair to keep it out of my eyes, and in the older nurse who said she and other nurses would be keeping watch through the night just outside my door. I also heard it in the voice of the nurse who talked me through the night when I had pneumonia and found it difficult to breathe.

It happened after I got home, when I was beginning to recover and feeling impatient that things weren't going faster. It happened when I was feeling depressed and indifferent, not caring a lot about anything. It was a great time for the devil to attack.

My theology isn't big on the devil, but I recognize an enemy who "prowls around like a roaring lion, looking for someone to devour" (1 Peter 5:8). I've watched enough nature shows to know that lions are quick to attack the vulnerable—the young, the old, the sick. Therefore, I shouldn't have been surprised that I was attacked when I was at my most vulnerable.

For one of the first times in my life, I was tempted to lose faith, to despair, to give up. I was too centered on myself, and the more I was, the less I was aware of my progress. My relationship with God weakened, and I wasn't as eager to read the Bible or pray or write in my journal as I normally was.

Again, I responded by talking with my ministers and an elder who visited me in the hospital and at home. I admitted my struggles, and they prayed with and for me.

I asked for the prayers of the church, which already had been praying for my physical recovery. It gave me comfort to know that these people, even in my absence, were thinking about me and keeping me in their prayers.

As soon as I was able, I rejoined them. I had to use a walker that first Sunday, and I hated and was embarrassed by it, but I went anyway. It was too important just to be there, to sing and pray and listen to the sermon. Our minister, Mark Manassee, was preaching a series on prayer, and his sermon, titled "Help," seemed written just for me.

He told us to be encouraged and strengthened by God's word, quoting 2 Corinthians 4:16-18: "Therefore we do not lose heart. Though outwardly we are wasting away, yet inwardly we are being renewed day by day. For our light and momentary troubles are achieving for us an eternal glory that far outweighs them all. So we fix our eyes not on what is seen, but on what is unseen. For what is seen is temporary, but what is unseen is eternal."

He encouraged us to be strengthened by the Holy Spirit and by our church family. He urged us to test our own actions, but not to compare them with others. And he told us to seek to please the Spirit; and not to grow weary, but to do good to all, especially our church family.

He said nothing I didn't already know, but he reminded me of things I needed to think about. I had to get back to praying, reading, meditating on Scripture, and writing in my journal.

One passage of Scripture that spoke to me was Psalm 1:1-3: "Blessed is the man who does not walk in the counsel of the wicked or stand in the way of sinners or sit in the seat of mockers. But his delight is in the law of the Lord, and on his law he meditates day and night. He is like a tree planted by streams of water, which yields its fruit in season and whose leaf does not wither. Whatever he does prospers."

When I meditate on God's Word, I find continual refreshment. I can feel the energy flow from my eyes to my mind and through my body to the tips of my fingers. I feel refreshed and renewed, no matter how withered my body is becoming.

"Blessed are those who hunger and thirst for righteousness, for they will be filled" (Matthew 5:6). We need to desire God as we desire food when we're hungry.

And Colossians 1:9-13: "We have not stopped praying for you and asking God to fill you with the knowledge of his will through all spiritual wisdom and understanding . . . being strengthened with all power according to his glorious might so that you may have great endurance and patience, and joyfully giving thanks to the Father, who has qualified you to share in the inheritance of the saints in the kingdom of light. For he has rescued us from the dominion of darkness and brought us into the kingdom of the son he loves, in whom we have redemption, the forgiveness of sins."

As I renewed my ties both to the church and to my own devotions, I began to feel that filling, that strengthening, that patience and joyful thanksgiving, that certainty of having been rescued, redeemed, and forgiven.

That was the time one of my sisters at Culver Palms told me about the Culver City Nature Trail, a twenty-minute walk operated by the Baldwin Hills conservancy that takes you up 105 feet. It is a wooden walkway that climbs gradually up the western side of the Baldwin Hills in a series of switchbacks. Frank and I climbed it together, and on the way up, the sky was clear. We could see the Santa Monica Mountains, the Hollywood Hills, the ocean, and more.

We located our house, or rather the studio at the end of our block, and the new rainbow installation that curves over it.

The next Sunday, I was back at worship, but without my walker.

The week that our class talked about spiritual health, Vicenta Jacobs spoke to us about it. Vicenta is known as a person of prayer. She is one of the few women I know who really enjoys silent retreats (though she likes to talk as much as most of us do). She guided our thoughts, urging us to be encouraged and strengthened in three ways:

1 By His Word—Vicenta used the scripture that Mark had used my first Sunday back: "Therefore we do not lose heart.... For our light and momentary troubles are achieving for us an eternal glory that far outweighs them all. So we fix our eyes not on what is seen, but on what is unseen, since what is seen is temporary, but what is unseen is eternal" (2 Corinthians 4:16-18). I assumed there was a message there for me—having been told twice that my troubles were "light and momentary."

She said, "Our focus is our inward renewal. Our present life is for a purpose in the next life. We fix our eyes on the unseen and the eternal as we live out our life daily."

2 By the Holy Spirit—"You, however, are controlled not by the sinful nature but by the Spirit, if the Spirit of God lives in you. And if anyone does not have the Spirit of Christ, he does not belong to Christ. But if Christ is in you, your body dead because of sin, yet your spirit is alive because of righteousness. And if the Spirit of him who raised Jesus from the dead is living in you, he who raised Christ from the dead will also give life to your mortal bodies through his Spirit, who lives in you" (Romans 8:9-11).

She urged us to "Call on him and wait for his wisdom, power, and directing."

3 By our church family—"Carry each other's burdens, and in this way you will fulfill the law of Christ. If anyone thinks he

is something when he is nothing, he deceives himself. Each one should test his own actions. Then he can take pride in himself, without comparing himself to somebody else, for each one should carry his own load" (Galatians 6:2-5).

And "Do not be deceived: God cannot be mocked. A man reaps what he sows. The one who sows to please his sinful nature, from that nature will reap destruction; the one who sows to please the Spirit, from the Spirit will reap eternal life. Let us not become weary in doing good, for at the proper time we will reap a harvest if we do not give up. Therefore, as we have opportunity, let us do good to all people, especially to those who belong to the family of believers" (Galatians 6:7-10).

Vicenta encouraged us to "Ask for help. Be available to serve."

We listed in our journals three things (one on each point) that we might like to do to grow closer to God, to His church, and to the world around us. I subscribed to an online Bible reading service that sends a section of Scripture to my inbox each morning. I asked for prayers and made a point of talking with others who did the same, letting them know I was praying for them and doing what I could to be of practical help. I also added items from the news to my prayers, asking God's help and seeking wisdom for those working directly with the situations.

As I began to improve in 2013, I wrote a website at *billiesilvey. com* on "Planning for Retirement." In it, I discussed planning in terms of physical, mental, and emotional health.

Then I began writing the curriculum for the Bible class called "Growing Old with Christ." I taught it that summer.

To maintain spiritual health, you'll want to read the Bible and pray, worship with your local church, and have your own private devotions. You'll want to think about God and His will, in general and for you specifically, and to live as consistently as you can with what you understand that will to be.

You'll want to love other people and to do good for them as you're able. You'll want to look for the good in people and situations. You'll want to be joyful and grateful and to express that joy and gratitude to God and to the people around you.

That fall, Mark preached a sermon series on Revelation. I put together a notebook with art from the Internet illustrating key verses and with notes on the sermons. I felt my spiritual health returning as I saw the vision of God in heaven, of Jesus walking among the candlesticks, and John writing his letters to the churches. Even the beasts had a meaning they'd lacked in the past.

But the symbol that spoke most to me was Jesus, the Lamb that was slain. Through His suffering, my salvation was made possible, and through my suffering, I was able to identify with Him and seek to help others.

The book ends with the "river of the water of life, as clear as crystal, flowing from the throne of God and of the Lamb down the middle of the great street of the city. On each side of the river stood the tree of life.... And the leaves of the tree are for the healing of the nations" (Revelation 22:1-3).

The leaves were for my healing as well, as they were among the ways I've been able to recover, and maintain, my spiritual health during my victory lap.

Discussion Questions

1. What do you do to maintain spiritual health?
2. How can you grow closer to God?
3. How can you grow closer to His church?
4. How can you grow closer to the world around you?
5. Where do we find continual refreshment for our spirits?
6. What three ways are we strengthened?

Bible Study

1. "Therefore we do not lose _____. Though outwardly we are _____ _____, yet inwardly we are being _____ day by day. So we fix our eyes not on what is _____, but on what is _____. For what is seen is _____, but what is unseen is _____" (2 Corinthians 4:16-18).

2. "Blessed is the man who does not walk in the counsel of the _____ or stand in the way of _____ or sit in the seat of _____. But his delight is in the _____ of the Lord, and on his law he

_____ day and night (Psalm 1:2).

3. "We have not stopped _____for you and asking

   God to fill you with the knowledge of his will through all spiritual

   _____ and _____. . .

   being _____ with all power according to his

   glorious _____ " (Colossians 9:13).

4. "You, however, are controlled not by the sinful nature but by the

   _____, if the _____ of God lives in

   you. And if anyone does not have the _____ of

   Christ, he does not belong to Christ. But if Christ is in you, your body

   is _____ because of sin, yet your _____

   is alive because of righteousness." (Romans 8:9-11).

5. "_____ each other's _____, and in this

   way you will fulfill the law of Christ" (Galatians 6:2).

6. "Do not be deceived: God cannot be mocked. A man

   _____ what he _____.The one who

   sows to please his sinful nature, from that nature will reap

   _____; the one who sows to please the Spirit,

   from the Spirit will reap _____ _____ "

   (Galatians 6:7).

Write in Your Journal

List in your journal three things (one on each point) that you might do to grow closer to God, to His church, and to the world around you.

Endnotes

22 http://cas.umkc.edu/casww/sa/spirituality.htm.

23 http://www.merckmanuals.com/professional/geriatrics/social_issues_in_the_elderly/ religion_and_spirituality_in_the_elderly.html.

CHAPTER 7

How Can We Maintain A Support Network?

When I was in the hospital for my surgery, having a shunt put into my skull, my husband, Frank, and my children, Kathy and Robert, visited often. I remember once waking up in the night to find that Robert had been sleeping on the couch in my room. A light was shining in from the street, and it was such a comfort to see his 6'3" frame rise up against it.

Kathy even brought six-year-old Katyana, who drew pictures on a little table in the room. The nurses posted her drawings on the wall, where I could see them from my bed. She also went with her grandfather, a UCLA graduate, to explore the campus. She especially enjoyed the sculpture garden and the students who were making a movie and let her use the clapper to start a scene.

Our ministers visited, talked, and prayed with me, expressing a real interest in how I was doing—not just physically, but on many levels.

When I got home after the surgery and had a seizure, Robert called the paramedics, located my insurance card, and got me back into the hospital. He probably saved my life.

And the horrible night I couldn't breathe from pneumonia, a young nurse stayed by my bedside, encouraging me to keep breathing.

During and after the time I taught the class on "Growing Old with God," I enjoyed four special events.

The first was the trip to Monterey that I hadn't been able to make the year before because I'd just had surgery. Frank and I took care of Katyana while Kathy taught and attended sessions of her English professors' conference. We rested, went to the park for a picnic, toured the aquarium, watched the sun set over the ocean, and ate at Fisherman's Wharf to the sound of barking sea lions. It was a treasured family time.

The next month, we returned to the Monterey area for the Silvey family reunion at Asilomar, a YWCA camp now managed as a California state park and beach. Thirty people—Frank and his five brothers and sisters, and their children and grandchildren—hiked, swam, golfed, or just rested and watched the wildlife. It was a great time of celebration and singing and sharing with the extended family.

Then, on August 25, Frank and I celebrated our 50th wedding anniversary at our home congregation, which I described in the previous chapter.

This summer, one of Frank's brothers rented a villa at Castel Gandolfo in Italy to celebrate his retirement. He and his wife had the whole family over, a week at a time, to visit. That was a real high point. All five of us—Kathy, Katyana, Robert, Frank, and

I—went to relax at the villa and sightsee in Rome and Paris.

It's important to have people around who care about you. We all need support networks made up of family, friends, neighbors, church family, and health care professionals—and we also need to be support networks for one another. There are several verses in Scripture that tell us that.

One is Ecclesiastes 4:9-12: "Two are better than one, because they have a good return for their work: If one falls down, his friend can help him up. But pity the man who falls and has no one to help him up! Also, if two lie down together, they will keep warm. But how can one keep warm alone? Though one may be overpowered, two can defend themselves. A cord of three strands is not quickly broken."

My family are my closest friends. It's a real comfort to know that I'll always have someone to pick me up, to keep me warm, and to defend me.

My sister, Barbara, and I have had trouble getting together the past few years because of health issues we've both had, but we visit often by phone or email. Her continued love has encouraged me all my life, especially since our parents died.

Paul, in Ephesians 4:11-13, points out that Jesus "gave some to be apostles, some to be prophets, some to be evangelists, and some to be pastors and teachers, to prepare God's people for works of service, so that the body of Christ may be built up until we all reach unity in the faith and in the knowledge of the Son of God and become mature, attaining to the whole measure of the fullness of Christ."

When I was ill, my home congregation was a constant support as they visited, sent gifts and cards, and prayed for me.

And Hebrews 3:12-13 speaks of the importance of encouragement: "See to it brothers, that none of you has a sinful, unbelieving heart that turns away from the living God. But encourage one another daily, as long as it is called Today, so that none of you may be hardened by sin's deceitfulness."

I have been so blessed in my various church homes over the years. I recall with gratitude wonderful leaders who inspired me in my first church home in Happy, Texas; during my college career in Abilene and Los Angeles; and since.

At the Vermont Avenue church, Bill and Ruby Green were special friends, teachers, and mentors, as were Michio and Lorraine Nagai and Norvel and Helen Young. Betty Bridges and Elsie Tatum were personal friends who have continued to encourage.

At Culver Palms, I've been built up by the preaching of Mark Manassee and Ron Cox. Elders Bernie James, Keith Brisco, and Greg McNair have encouraged my service. Rona Kingsley and Toby Considine are special friends. And hundreds of Christians in both churches have worked with me, encouraging me to worship and serve.

Keith Brisco is one of the best encouragers I know. He encouraged me when I first began worshipping at Culver Palms to attend the small group that met in his home. He's encouraged me over the years by participating with enthusiasm in projects I've taken on, like our booth at the Culver City Community Fair and Culver Palms Life Skills Lab. He encouraged me by being one of my first visitors when I got home from the hospital and just by attending the class I taught on growing old.

Rona Kingsley has one of the largest support networks of anyone I've ever known. I got to know her well when she volunteered to help me in the office with Life Skills Lab. She's upbeat and looks for things she can do to make things better.

She worked sitting across the desk from me, and one day as she sat there, she started thinking about ways to rearrange the furniture in our tiny office to maximize the space and make the room look larger. But she didn't just think. She jumped up and started moving furniture.

What have other people done for you? What can you do for other people?

There are people in all our lives who lift us, and there are others who bring us down. Who in your life lifts your spirits and gives you encouragement? How can you make friends who can be a positive support? How can you be a positive support for others? And what can you do to help those "downers," who are hurting themselves more than they're hurting anybody else with their negative attitudes?

Write in your journal the names of people who encourage you, and when you get a chance, thank them for it. Also, write the names of those who need your encouragement and list a couple of steps you can take to give it.

As we grow older, our friends and family members take on renewed importance. We find ourselves re-establishing contact with old friends with whom we've lost touch. At our anniversary party, Bonnie Leitch, a friend from elementary and high school in Happy, came from Texas to celebrate with us. It was a huge surprise. Another surprise was the presence of Kay Burton Nagle, a friend from Abilene Christian who just happened to be in the city, and Betty and Joe Bridges, friends from the Vermont Avenue church who now live in the Valley.

It's important that we maintain our support group as we grow older. We may need to rediscover people with whom we've lost touch. We can do that online through Google, through mutual friends, and through organizations like alumni associations.

Once we're in touch, it's important to maintain that connection through letters, cards, phone calls. and email. Get together, whenever possible, to keep that connection strong. Sustain contact with church friends by taking part in church activities and through other means of contact. Endeavor to visit neighbors from time to time or to invite them over.

An article in *Renew*, the magazine of United Healthcare, tells us that good friends can be as important to our health as a good diet and regular exercise.[24] Socializing boosts our immune system and helps fight depression. A 2008 Harvard School of Public Health study "showed that an active social life slows older adults' memory loss."

The article suggests activities that combine socializing with "something that occupies your mind and body," like game nights, walking and talking with a friend, making music together, tackling a new activity, learning to dance, or bowling with friends.

My husband, Frank, has a wonderful circle of supportive friends who are members of his vocal group, the Mansfield Chamber Singers. I know they keep him active and involved in doing something he loves with a group of people he cares about and who care about him.

Unfortunately, as I grow older, my circle of friends is growing older, too. They are beginning to suffer various physical difficulties, just as I am. I find myself visiting them in the hospital, sending more get-well cards and sympathy cards than ever before.

This year, Steven Mittleman, our valued family physician, who was just ten years older than our daughter, died. That was a shock on several levels, as he'd done a lot to keep me healthy and alive.

Robert Browning, the Victorian poet and son of a devout evangelical Christian, wrote the following:

Grow old along with me!

The best is yet to be,

The last of life, for which the first was made:

Our times are in His hand

Who saith "A whole I planned,

Youth shows but half; trust God: see all, nor be afraid!"

I want to make a point of staying in touch with family and friends, both here and in other places. I know that, as I grow older, the people in my life are increasingly important to me. I want to continue to function as a support for them. I want to be open to people I don't know so well with an eye toward expanding my circle of friends. And I also want to continue meeting and making friends of people who are younger than I am. Only by making new, younger friends can I ensure that my support network will continue through my life.

Discussion Questions

1. Who are the people in your immediate and extended family who are part of your support group? How can you grow closer?

2. Who are the people in your church who are part of your support group? How can you get to know them better?

3. What friends and neighbors are in your support group? How can you extend that group?

4. With which friends can you re-establish contact? What can you do to reconnect with them? (I searched online for one old friend, and we were able to re-establish contact.)

5. What can you do to expand your circle and make younger friends?

6. How do friends and family members help us maintain good health?

Bible Study

1. "_____ are better than _____, because they have a good return for their work: If one _____ _____, his friend can _____ him _____" (Ecclesiastes 4:9-12).

2. "He gave some to be _____, some to be

_____, and _____, so that

the _____ of _____ may be built

up until we all reach _____ in the faith and in

the _____ of the Son of God and become

_____, attaining to the whole measure of the

_____ of Christ" (Ephesians 4:11-13).

3. "See to it brothers, that none of you has a sinful, unbelieving heart

that turns away from the _____ _____.

But _____ one another daily, as long as it is called

_____, so that none of you may be hardened by sin's

deceitfulness" (Hebrews 3:12-13).

Write in Your Journal

Write in your journal the names of people who encourage you. Write them a note to thank them. Also, write the name of a person you can encourage together with two or three specific suggestions for doing so that you can implement over the next few weeks.

Endnotes

24 https://www.uhcmedicaresolutions.com/pdf/ma_svn/UHC_Renew_Newsletter_MA_MAPD.pdf.

CHAPTER 8

How Can We Stay Active and Involved?

When I first got out of the hospital, we had been trying to refinance our house. That came through the second week I was home. I co-signed all the papers and did what I could to understand our new commitments.

I went back to church. I'm always happier when I'm active and involved with a faith community.

I wrote thank-you notes to people who had sent reminders of their care. Gratitude is a positive emotion that helps us stay active and involved. It is good for us to express our gratitude to one another and to God.

I finished filling out a book Katyana had given me to write memories in for her, and I started working on an album of family photographs. It's important to re-assess our lives and realize what we have accomplished, particularly when we're able to accomplish less.

I cleaned the house and read a lot. Orderly surroundings make me feel more comfortable, and reading stimulates my mind.

The first weekend of the second month, we babysat Katyana

while Kathy attended a conference for English professors, and I sent get-well cards to a couple of friends. It's important not just to accept kindnesses; I needed to do what I could to help and encourage those around me—even my own family.

I got my wedding ring resized after they had had to cut it off for an MRI. After fifty years of marriage, it had become embedded in my finger. It was also embedded in my heart, and that empty ring finger, with the deep indentation encircling it, made me sad. It felt good to have it back where it belonged.

It was easy, after I'd spent time in the hospital with others supplying my every need, to want to extend the pampering after I got home, to want to continue resting and being cared for. But it was important to get up and get involved.

According to an article by Cecily Fraser of CBS, eighty percent of retirees plan to work at least part time.[25] "People will begin living a cyclical life plan, go back to school, cease their major career and re-invent themselves," said Ken Dychwald, an author of books on health and aging issues. "People will pursue freedom, not retirement."

When I first retired, I didn't experience it as freedom, but as boredom. Even though I hadn't died, I felt as though my usefulness had. No one was expecting me and my talents to show up anywhere to contribute to getting things done. I scarcely felt like doing even the basic tasks of caring for myself.

The top ten ways of remaining active after retirement, according to Fraser, include: traveling, family activities, hobbies, gardening, fishing, golfing, volunteering, reading, exercising and home improvement.

According to a U.S. Bureau of Labor Statistics news release on volunteering in the U.S., about twenty-four percent of those 65 and over, volunteer.[26] Thirty-three per cent volunteer with religious organizations; 25.6% with educational or youth services; and 14.7%, with social or community service organizations. Activities include collecting, preparing, distributing or serving food (10.9%), fundraising (10.0%), and tutoring or teaching (9.8%). The more education a person has, the more likely he or she is to volunteer.

I did entirely too much sitting—in front of the computer, in front of the TV, and on the couch reading. I was taking my walks on most days, but I didn't feel much motivation or energy to do more. Mostly, I didn't feel needed.

Frank and I figure that we each took between six months and a year just sitting and taking stock after we retired. In my case, I still had recovery to do. But we each hit a point when we were rested and ready to get back to work again. It was just a question of what direction we wanted to go and what most needed to be done. Only now, more than two years later, are we actively seeking projects that are the best use of the time we have left.

Currently, we are organizing family photographs to have them in good order, with captions explaining who, what, when, and where the events occurred. We continue putting up the website, and I'm also teaching teenagers in Bible class.

Scripture points to the importance of being active and involved. It tells us to "respect those who work hard among you, who are over you in the Lord and who admonish you. Hold them in the highest regard in love because of their work. Live in peace with each other. And we urge you, brothers, warn those who are idle, encourage the timid, help the weak, be patient with everyone. Make sure that nobody pays back wrong for wrong, but always try to be kind to each other and to everyone else.

"Be joyful always; pray continually; give thanks in all circumstances, for this is God's will for you in Christ Jesus" (1 Thessalonians 5:12-18).

The book of Proverbs is full of exhortations to activity: "How long will you lie there, you sluggard? When will you get up from your sleep? A little sleep, a little slumber, a little folding of the hands to rest—and poverty will come on you like a bandit and scarcity like an armed man" (Proverbs 6:9-11).

"Finish your outdoor work and get your fields ready; after that, build your house" (Proverbs 24:27).

It points out the ridiculous extremes to which we may go to justify laziness: "The sluggard says, 'There is a lion in the road, a fierce lion roaming the streets!'" But the writer of Proverbs isn't fooled by our excuses: "As a door turns on its hinges, so a sluggard turns on his bed. The sluggard buries his hand in the dish; he is too lazy to bring it back to his mouth" (Proverbs 26:13-15).

The writer of Ecclesiastes encourages us to "Sow your seed in the morning, and at evening let not your hands be idle, for you do not know which will succeed, whether this or that, or whether both will do equally well" (Ecclesiastes 11:6).

And the psalmist shows the natural progression of activity on earth: "The moon marks off the seasons, and the sun knows when to go down. You bring darkness, it becomes night, and all the beasts of the forest prowl. The lions roar for their prey and seek their food from God. The sun rises, and they steal away; they return and lie down in their dens. Then man goes out to his work, to his labor until evening" (Psalm 104:19-23).

At some point, we have to retire from our jobs, but there's no need to retire from life. In fact, it's counterproductive. We need to stay active and involved. I drew a web diagram of things I might enjoy doing, and each member of the class I was teaching on "Growing Old with God" did the same. We wrote the word *Activities* in the center of a sheet of paper, drew a circle around it, and drew lines out from the circle to words like *Physical, Mental, Social,* and other areas of interest. We circled those words and drew lines out from them to words like "walking," "reading," and "inviting a friend to lunch."

This diagram can grow out in all directions to help you think of useful and interesting activities for your retirement. We discussed things we'd done in the past that brought joy and added them to the chart.

Kelly Shaw, an occupational therapist, was the professional expert for the class on this topic. Kelly is the wife of one of our song leaders and the mother of Sydney and Austin, two of Katyana's friends. She talked about physical and occupational therapists and the work they do to insure that people remain active and involved.

I talked about the physical therapist who came to my house, and I demonstrated the stretching exercises he taught me that I continue doing today.

We wrote in our journals about new activities we could explore as well as treasured activities we wanted to continue doing.

A member of the benevolence committee at church, I went back it on September 1 for my first meeting of the group that provides financial and food aid to those who need. This was followed by two meetings in October. It was coming up on Thanksgiving and Christmas, our busiest times of the year, and I wanted to get involved again.

As my health improved, I got more involved, and as I became more involved, my health improved. It's what is called a "virtuous cycle."

I had received an assignment to write three articles for *Power for Today*, the daily devotional guide. They were due October 1, and I started them, writing on topics that were significant to me in my recovery.

It encouraged me to be trusted with these assignments, and it encouraged me to research and meditate and write on the topics of God's faithfulness and our limitations, but the need to do what we can, trusting his provision.

In November, I worked with the Benevolence Committee to

gather food to distribute to those in need. And on Thanksgiving Day, I baked a turkey for our family feast. It had been almost a year and a half since my surgery, and I was grateful to be able to do it.

In December, I was able to watch my granddaughter, Katyana, perform in *Mamma Mia*, where she sang "Honey, Honey," and in South Bay Ballet's performance of *The Nutcracker* at El Camino College, where she was the cutest Bow Mouse. (Grandmothers aren't partial.) On Christmas Eve, I hosted our traditional *hors d'oeuvres* supper and gift opening here. Then, on Christmas Day, we went down to Kathy's to see Katyana's gifts and have dinner there. It had been a great year of recovery and growing involvement with life. It had been a real victory lap.

But activity and involvement is not just a one-time thing. It needs to continue throughout your life. Here are some suggestions of ways you might stay active and involved as you continue to age:

1. You can stop periodically to evaluate where you are, what you are able to do, and how your interests are changing. Think over or even list what you're doing. Are you getting tired all the time? Bored? Satisfied? Do you need to drop some activities or add others, or is your activity level just about right for your level of energy?

2. You can remain curious, researching new ways to participate in life and activities. The Internet has to be the greatest advance to the curious person.

3. You can accept the opportunities that come your way and even volunteer occasionally.

4. You can be interested and aware of what needs doing—particularly of what needs your prayers and participation.

5. You can continue doing those tasks that are within your realm of responsibility, things that need to be done around the house and among your circle of family and friends.

6. You can look for ways to continue using your gifts to serve others.

7. You can seek new interests and new topics to learn. Even when you're watching TV, you can opt for programs that will enrich and challenge you.

The more active and involved you are with life, the better able you'll be to stay physically, mentally, emotionally, and spiritually healthy. Consequently, you'll experience more joy, peace, and satisfaction in your victory laps.

Discussion Questions

1. What are some ways you can become more active and involved during your victory lap?

2. What are the advantages of being involved with a faith-based community or church?

3. How can you show more gratitude to God and to other people?

4. How can you help others?

5. How can you distinguish between actual physical limitations and laziness?

6. What are some things you've done in the past that have brought joy? How many of them can you continue or adapt to your current situation?

Bible Study

1. "_____ those who work hard among you, who are over you in the Lord and who _____ you. Hold them in the _____ regard in love because of their work. Live in _____ with each other. . . . Warn those who are _____, encourage the _____, help the _____, be _____ with everyone. (1 Thessalonians 5:12-14).

2. Be _____ always, _____ continually, give _____ in all circumstances, for this is _____ _____ for you in

_____ _____

(1 Thessalonians 5:16-18).

3. "How long will you _____ there you _____? When will you get up from your _____? A little _____, a little _____, a little folding of the hands to _____ — and poverty will come on you like a _____ and scarcity like an

_____ _____" (Proverbs 6:9-11).

4. "The _____ says, There is a _____ in the

_____, a fierce _____ roaming the

_____ " (Proverbs 26:13).

5. "The _____ marks off the _____, and

the _____ knows when to go down. You bring

_____, it becomes _____, and all the

beasts of the forest prowl. The _____ roar for their

_____ and seek their _____ from God.

The _____ rises, and they steal away; they return and

lie down in their dens. Then _____ goes out to his

_____, and to his _____ until evening"

(Psalm 104:19-23).

6. "_____ your seed in the morning, and at evening, do not

let your _____ be _____, for you do not know

which will succeed, whether this or that, or whether both will do

equally well" (Ecclesiastes 11:6).

Write in Your Journal

Draw a web diagram of activities you could begin to take part in today.

Endnotes

25 http://www.marketwatch.com/story/top-10-most-desired-retirement-activities.

26 http://www.bls.gov/news.release/volun.nr0.htm.

CHAPTER 9

How Can We Prepare for Death?

After my illness, I found myself thinking often about death. In a sense, I'd thought about death all my life. As a Christian, I knew what the Bible said about dying and being with Jesus. And as an admirer of the Romantic movement in poetry, I'd always expected to die young. But this was different. I was old, and my illness made me suddenly aware of the reality of death. I was frightened.

I tried to imagine a world without myself, but I couldn't, because I've always been here in my consciousness. I realized how poorly prepared I was for facing death. It's one of the sure things in life for each of us, and yet we seldom discuss it.

On April 15, 2013, *The Los Angeles Times* ran two separate articles about preparing for death. The first was about Elliot Kharkats, a West Los Angeles man who put a chalkboard on his back gate so people could fill in one thing they'd like to do before they die. A list of such things is called a bucket list and was popularized by a film by the same name starring Jack Nicholson and Morgan Freeman. I enjoyed the movie and had considered drafting such a list—when I got old. Suddenly, I felt old, and I wasn't sure I wanted to create such a list.

I've since discovered that a bucket list can be valuable in giving you something to look forward to. First, I looked forward to our trip to Italy. After that, I plan to write the story of my life, even if only for my family.

Another article in the same issue was on Betsy Trapasso, who lives in Topanga Canyon and who hosted Los Angeles's first Death Cafe. That's a movement that began in England where people, often strangers, gather to eat cake, drink tea and discuss death.

Death is a subject most people avoid discussing. "My whole thing is to get people talking about it so they're not afraid when the time comes," says Trapasso, who was a hospice social worker in the early days of the hospice movement in Los Angeles.

I've always felt it was important to talk about death. It comes to all, and facing it helps keep me real and facing reality. Also, it gives a special urgency to my victory lap. I don't have all the time in the world to do those things that are important to me—loving my family and friends, staying in touch with extended family and friends from the past, completing projects that are important to me, and dropping some that aren't so important. It helps me clarify my priorities.

How much thought have you given to death? It's going to happen someday. Two years ago, I thought that I was dying on three different occasions. I count the past two years, and any more time God sees fit to give me, as the "victory lap" Margaret talked about in the first lesson.

It's also an opportunity to prepare to do the things on my bucket list and to express my wishes about end-of-life issues.

In *Fountain of Age,* Betty Friedan[27] quotes a Harris Poll that only eight percent of Americans over 65 identify themselves as being old. "A majority also objected to 'older American,' 'golden-ager,' 'old-timer,' 'aged person' or even 'middle-aged person.' Barely half accepted the term 'senior citizen,' 'mature American' or 'retired person' for themselves." Friedan noted how some senior citizen clubs fine their members if they use the word "old."

But I am retired, and I am old. I hate all those euphemisms people employ to keep from just coming out and saying it. I particularly hate phrases with the words "silver" or "golden" in them.

David Hackett Fischer,[28] in *Growing Old in America,* talks about the cultural shift at the end of the eighteenth century from veneration to condescension when talking about old people. Contempt for age was expressed in labels like gaffer, fogey, codger, and fuddy-duddy.

It matters what we call ourselves as we grow older. It matters because it influences the way we see ourselves and thus, the way we relate to others. If I refuse to see myself as old or retired, I'm saying there's something a little shameful about that fact. I'm letting the culture around me dictate who I am rather than the God who made and loves me.

According to the CDC,[29] since 1900, life expectancy in the U.S. has dramatically increased, and the principal causes of death have changed. At the beginning of the twentieth century, many Americans died young. Most did not live to the age of 65, their lives often abruptly ended by one of a variety of infectious diseases.

My grandfather, Mose Wesley, died in the influenza epidemic of 1918 when my father was still a baby and Granny was expecting my Aunt Maxine. My grandfather's brother and a cousin died around the same time—all three young men with their lives just beginning.

Today, about seventy-five percent of all deaths are among people who are 65 or older. The majority are caused by such chronic conditions as heart disease, cancer, stroke, diabetes, and Alzheimer's disease.

God knows that death is fearful, and He comforts us with the words of the psalmist: "Even though I walk through the valley of the shadow of death, I will fear no evil, for you are with me; your rod and your staff they comfort me. You prepare a table before me in the presence of my enemies. You anoint my head with oil; my cup overflows. Surely goodness and love will follow me all the days of my life, and I will dwell in the house of the LORD forever" (Psalm 23:4-6).

God urges us not to fear death, but to approach it with trust in His presence, comfort, and provision. God has wonderful blessings for us as we run our victory laps. Our cups really can overflow with them. We have the promise of His presence with us as we move through death to the other side.

And Jesus said: "Do not let your hearts be troubled. Trust in God; trust also in me. In my Father's house are many rooms; if it were not so, I would have told you. I am going there to prepare a place for you. And if I go and prepare a place for you, I will come back and take you to be with me that you also may be where I am. You know the way to the place where I am going…. I am the way and the truth and the life. No one comes to the Father except through me" (John 14:1-6).

These verses seem to indicate a particular place. Just where it is or what it's like doesn't matter much to me. The key, for me, is Jesus' words, "that you also may be where I am." In the 1940s, there was a popular song called "My Happiness." My family used to harmonize as we sang it together. The words speak of being happy "any place on earth, just as long as I'm with you."

That's the way I feel about Jesus. So long as I'm with Him, I'll be happy.

"Listen, I tell you a mystery: We will not all sleep, but we will all be changed—in a flash, in the twinkling of an eye, at the last trumpet. For the trumpet will sound, the dead will be raised imperishable, and we will be changed…then the saying that is written will come true: 'Death has been swallowed up in victory'" (1 Corinthians 15:51-54).

It's going to be different after death. I'm going to be different. I don't understand what it's going to be like, but I know that it's going to be good. Death is a victory. It is something to anticipate, not fear. It is the natural culmination of life.

"For I am convinced that neither death nor life, neither angels nor demons, neither the present nor the future, nor any powers, neither height nor depth, nor anything else in all creation, will be able to separate us from the love of God that is in Christ Jesus our Lord" (Romans 8:38-39).

Death, like life, is under God's control, in His presence, and in His love. It's the result of God's love. God's love has already been expressed for us in the death of Jesus. He's given His best for us, and even death won't separate us from His love.

"For to me, to live is Christ and to die is gain" (Philippians 1:21).

Whatever my future holds, I can rest secure that it holds good, victory, and God's love for me.

And Paul tells us to encourage one another in the face of death: "We believe that Jesus died and rose again and so we believe that God will bring with Jesus those who have fallen asleep in him.... For the Lord himself will come down from heaven, with a loud command, with the voice of the archangel and with the trumpet call of God, and the dead in Christ will rise first. After that, we who are still alive and are left will be caught up together with them in the clouds to meet the Lord in the air. And so we will be with the Lord forever. Therefore encourage each other with these words" (1 Thessalonians 4:14-18).

It's obvious that whatever happens will happen quickly, that we will be changed, that we will continue in God's love and presence, that death will be gain, and that we will be with Him forever. I may not understand just what that means, but I know that it means good, and I should be encouraged.

Finally, Revelation has always been a book that encourages me. Our minister, Mark Manassee, had just finished his series of sermons, Bible classes, and growth group discussions of the book of Revelation when I began writing this book.

I especially loved the concluding lines of the letters to the churches: "To him who overcomes, I will give the right to eat from the tree of life, which is in the paradise of God" (Revelation 2:7); "He who overcomes will not be hurt at all by the second death" (Revelation 2:11); "To him who overcomes, I will give some of the hidden manna. I will also give him a white stone with a new name written on it, known only to him who receives it" (Revelation 2:17); "To him who overcomes and does my will to the end, I will give authority over the nations—He will rule them with an iron scepter; he will dash them to pieces like pottery" (Revelation 2:26-27).

"He who overcomes will…be dressed in white. I will never blot out his name from the book of life, but will acknowledge his name before my Father and his angels" (Revelation 3:5); "Him who overcomes I will make a pillar in the temple of my God. Never again will he leave it. I will write on him the name of my God and the name of the city of my God, the new Jerusalem, which is coming down out of heaven from my God; and I will also write on him my new name" (Revelation 3:11-12); and "To him who overcomes, I will give the right to sit with me on my throne, just as I overcame and sat down with my Father on his throne" (Revelation 3:21).

I want to overcome. So I must overcome many things, but mostly myself and my tendency to give up, to grow discouraged, and to fear death.

The victory promised in these passages and the close relationship with God are a comfort to all who call on His name.

In the Bible class on death, we wrote in our journals the first three items on our bucket list. What three things would you like to do before you die?

When I knew I was ill, I thought back over my life and discovered that I'd done just about everything I'd wanted to do. I married a fine man with whom I'd shared fifty years. We have two great children we get to see almost every week. And I can't forget to mention our granddaughter, Katyana, who has brought such delight to our lives.

I love to study and learn new things, and I've been able to attend classes at ACU, Pepperdine, UCLA Extension and Fuller Seminary; I was even the first person in my family to graduate from college. I have, indeed, been blessed.

I love to write and to do things to help people. I've been able to spend the past sixty years working with words—on my dad's newspaper, doing publicity for Christian education, working as an editor and writer for *20th Century Christian Magazine*, and writing numerous books and articles for other publications.

I have also been able to work for a local church, start a nonprofit to help single parents get jobs, work for a nonprofit on the campus of an urban high school, and serve on the benevolence committee at church. I have been able to use my talents in ways that stretched me and helped other people.

I've even had the chance to travel abroad. By God's grace, little is left on my bucket list.

Until death comes, I plan to continue to learn, to write, to travel, and to make what contributions I can to the lives of others. After all, only the old can give the young the perspective they need on life. Only the old can see how past, present, and future interact and give the young a sense of it.

As Edmund Burke wrote in *Reflections on the Revolution in France,* "Society is a partnership not only between those who are living, but between those who are dead and those who are to be born." We owe a debt to past generations to remember them to the future, and we "owe those coming after us at least what we were given by those who came before us, the possibility of life and survival."

As we "pay it forward" to coming generations, we fulfill our need to live fully until our own deaths come.

Our minister's wife, Angela Manassee, is a hospice counselor. She spoke to our class when we studied about death.

We may need to organize our financial records, make health-care decisions, decide on the disposal of our bodies, consider our funeral or memorial service, or get emotional support. We may need to make some sort of record of our lives to share something of ourselves with those who come after.

Before I went into the hospital, I filled out UCLA's Advance

Health Care Directive. I asked for Frank or Kathy to serve as my agent to make decisions for me if I wasn't able. I expressed my choice about when to prolong life and my feelings about organ donation. Then I signed it in front of our son, Robert, and our neighbor, LaVergne. I had already drafted a simple will, including the kind of memorial service I'd prefer, and I asked our ministers and one of our song leaders to carry it out.

How can we prepare for death? The best way to prepare for death is to live life fully and joyfully until it comes. I want to live as close to God and as close to those special people in my life as I can. I want to live a life of service, a life of feeling involved with, and caring about the things that happen in the world.

I want to do what I can to seek peace among all people, to promote good—especially for the young, the weak, the poor, and the oppressed in life. I want to be God's person in this world, encouraging His aim of good for all people.

I want to bring order out of chaos—to organize my home, my desk, and my thoughts, so that I can live in clarity. I want to write or say something that will help make someone else's load lighter.

But the best way I've found to prepare for death is to trust God with it as I've trusted Him with my life since I gave it to Him in baptism when I was thirteen. He has always proved worthy of that trust. In fact, His guidance has always been better than what I might have thought I wanted myself. It's wonderful to relax and face whatever comes in Him.

Discussion Questions

1. Why do we have so much trouble facing the inevitability of death?

2. What could make it easier to feel prepared for death?

3. Name one thing on your bucket list, and explain why you want to do it before you die.

4. How can you act as a bridge between the generations that have gone before and those after you?

5. What level of end-of-life care do you want? (It can range all the way from no intervention to all possible efforts to maintain life.) Why did you select that level?

6. How do you feel about expressing your desires through a will and a living will?

Bible Study

1. "Even though I walk through the valley of the shadow of
_____, I will fear no _____, for _____
are with me, your _____ and your _____ they
comfort me" (Psalm 23:4).

2. "Do not let your hearts be _____.
_____ in God; _____ also in me. In my Father's
_____ are many _____ . . . . I am going
there to _____ a _____ for you. And if I
go and _____ a _____ for you,
I will _____ back and _____ you with me
that you also may be _____ I am" (John 14:1-3).

3. "Listen, I tell you a mystery: We will not all _____, but we will all be _____ — in a _____, in the _____ of an _____, at the last _____. For the _____ will sound, the _____ will be _____ imperishable, and we will be _____" (1 Corinthians 15:51-53).

4. "For I am convinced that neither _____ nor _____, neither _____ nor _____, nor any _____, neither _____ nor _____, nor anything else in all _____, will be able to _____ us from the _____ of God that is in _____ _____ our _____" (Romans 8:38-39).

5. "For to me, to _____ is _____ and to _____ is _____" (Philippians 1:21).

6. "For the Lord himself will come down from heaven, with a loud command, with the voice of the archangel and with the trumpet call of God, and the _____ in _____ will rise first. After that, we who are still _____ and left will be caught up with them in the _____ to meet the _____ in the air. And so we will be with the _____ forever. Therefore, _____ each other with these words" (1 Thessalonians 4:16-18).

Write in Your Journal

Write in your journal about your baptism and your subsequent life with God. Have you trusted God with your life? Has He proved faithful? Why shouldn't you trust God with your death as well?

Endnotes

27 https://www.trinity.edu/mkearl/gersopsy.html.

28 https://www.trinity.edu/mkearl/gersopsy.html.

29 http://www.cdc.gov/mmwr/preview/mmwrhtml/00056796.htm.

CHAPTER 10

What Is Your Legacy?

O ur house was built in 1926 by MGM Studios to house one of
their wardrobe designers—one of those who made the ruby
slippers Judy Garland wore. MGM sold it to the Heckman family,
and two generations of Heckmans lived here. Twenty years ago,
we began renting from the Heckmans with an option to buy. We
are only the third family to own the house in the eighty-eight years
of its existence. That must be some kind of record for L.A.

I fell in love with the house when I first saw it. It's a Spanish-
style bungalow with lots of windows; it's full of light. It has a big
backyard with four large trees that our granddaughter, Katyana,
has claimed as her own. It has survived earthquakes (one of
which damaged its chimney). But mostly, it's survived a lack of
proper care.

The first major work we had done on the house was to repair a
leaky roof. What a shock when the roofers discovered that there
was not just one—or even the three that the law allows—but
five roofs, one on top of the other! Rain could seep in between
the layers and end up emerging at a point in the house.

They tore them all off, making numerous trips to the dump, and replaced them with a single roof. We haven't had any leaks since.

Our next concern, living in Southern California, was earthquakes. Obviously the walls were sound, as they had already stood through a number of quakes, but we were concerned about the foundation.

The foundation specialist found that the house and the foundation were fine. They just weren't attached to each other. He remedied that situation.

More recently, the front porch had begun to sag and the sidewalk running to the driveway was cracked, so we called in a paver and porch repair expert. They discovered that the porch was extending from the front of the house over…absolutely nothing!

They built up a concrete base, topped it with a new porch and steps, and replaced the sidewalk. We had another workman install handrails at the front and back steps. At the time, I'd just had my surgery and was still having trouble with steps.

Until you start work on a house, you never know exactly what you have. We had a wonderful legacy of early Los Angeles, and now it is strong and sturdy and will survive for our children to live in, rent out, or sell.

Whatever they do with it, I'm grateful that we will be able to leave them something of solid value.

What kind of legacy will you leave when you die? Some people are able to leave generous sums of money to fund scholarships or build buildings in their memory, but most of us don't have enough money to make that sort of impact.

If you died tomorrow, who would inherit your house? Your belongings? Your family mementos?

According to a Harris poll published in 2013,[30] Sixty-one percent of all adult Americans do not have a will; seventy percent of Americans with children under 18 don't have one; and thirty-four percent of baby boomers (age 55-64) don't have one.[31] Their top three reasons for not having a will? Procrastination, a belief that they don't need one, and the cost involved. The real reason for not having a will? Not wanting to face the fact of death.

If you die intestate (without a will),[32] the state decides how your property is to be distributed. "You don't want the default to be what the state law happens to be," says estate planning lawyer Jason Smolen. "Sometimes it could work out in your favor, but sometimes it can't."[33]

Still, you will leave a legacy. How you live your life is the primary legacy you leave the world through those you've influenced. Jon Gordon points out that money is only one thing people leave behind: Some leave a legacy of excellence, others of encouragement, others of a purpose beyond themselves, and still others leave a legacy of love.[34]

What have you done in your life? For what are you known? Have you taught children or comforted the sorrowful or encouraged those who are discouraged? Have you fed the hungry or given a cup of cold water to those who thirst? Have you provided clothes or shelter to those who have lost theirs? Have you shown love to the neglected and lonely? To "the least of these"?

Dorcas was a woman in the Bible who left a notable legacy. We read about her in Acts 9:36-43. Dorcas's legacy was that she "was always doing good and helping the poor." When she died, the disciples sent for Peter, and when he came, "all the widows stood around him, crying and showing him the robes and other clothing that Dorcas had made while she was still with them."

What a wonderful legacy, to have done so much good that the widows brought out the garments she had made for them as a testimony to her life!

For many years, Jack Payne was responsible for the upkeep of our church building. He had owned a carpet cleaning business, and he kept the church building clean and well-repaired into his eighties. He loved church music and had a strong sense of God's grace. When he died, no one knew who to tell about plumbing problems, broken song-book racks, or stains on carpets. We all missed Jack because of his great legacy of service.

Our work can be our legacy. I had hoped that Life Skills Lab would continue as my legacy, what I would leave the world to make it a better place. But it wasn't to be the lasting legacy I'd hoped, though its influence continues among the scores we were able to serve.

Maria Shriver, in her *Inspirational Stories for Architects of Change*,[35] wrote about the legacy of Steve Jobs, in part because of the products he designed. But she also spoke of a friend's mother, a teacher, who was warm and welcoming, patient and kind, baked yummy treats for everyone in the neighborhood, and always had an open door at her home. "That was her legacy," Shriver pointed out, "how she touched other people's lives."

Shriver lists four lessons she feels will give life more meaning and make us happier and more fulfilled:

- Don't make money the end goal.

- Follow your passion.

- Learn to appreciate silence.

- Be nice.

Shriver's first point was reinforced by Jesus in His parable of the rich fool. Someone in the crowd that followed Jesus asked Him to tell his brother to divide his inheritance with him. Jesus responded with a warning against greed. He told of a rich man whose crops were so bountiful he ran out of places to store them. He planned to tear down his barns and build other ones and have plenty for many years of enjoyment. But Jesus said to him, "You fool! This very night your life will be demanded from you. Then who will get what you have prepared for yourself?" (Luke 12:20).

As Christians, it isn't just ourselves we should be concerned about, but others. Jesus tells us not to worry, but to lay up treasures for ourselves in heaven (Luke 12:33).

Helen Pepperdine was the wife of George Pepperdine who founded Pepperdine University. By the time I met her, she was growing old, but she still liked to do things with her hands.

She created a clown doll that she sold at the AWP Gift Fair.

We all wanted Helen Pepperdine clown dolls, and she must have sold thousands. I remember when Mrs. Pepperdine gave Kathy hers, and she told me recently that she still has it. The proceeds went toward scholarships for Christian students who otherwise couldn't afford to attend the college. Mrs. Pepperdine's husband may have founded the school, but she left a legacy in the lives of many who were educated there and in the joy her dolls brought to those who cherished them.

My greatest legacy is the two wonderful adults our children, Kathy and Robert, have grown up to be. They are kind, loving, and talented, and I'm so proud of them. And I see yet another legacy in our granddaughter, Katyana.

Other legacies are books I've written, classes I've taught, and even conversations I've had with people I hoped to influence for good.

I'm leaving items passed down to me from my grandparents with the hope that they'll be as meaningful to my children and grandchild as they have been to me. I've made scrapbooks and photo albums and have passed down family stories and traditions. And I'm leaving a love of literature and a love of God.

Even Jesus was aware of legacy. When He was in Bethany at the house of Simon the Leper, a woman brought an alabaster jar of perfume and poured it on his head. The story is in Mark 14:3-9. "I tell you the truth," he said, "wherever the gospel is preached throughout the world, what she has done will also be told, in memory of her."

And He Himself wanted to be remembered. That's why He left us the communion we as Christians share each week. "Do this in remembrance of me," he said (Luke 22:19).

When we talked about legacy in our Bible class, one of our elders, Greg McNair, came as a visiting expert. A lawyer for the Los Angeles Unified School District, Greg served with me on the board of Westchester Healthy Start. He also started a foundation to honor the memory of his in-laws, Homer F. and Marian G. Broome.

The Broome Foundation, according to its mission statement, "exists to equip and encourage young people and families through educational, legal, and support services, for lives of real value and significance—one young person and one family at a time." Greg is building a legacy through the lives of young people he serves.

He talked with the class about the legal documents we need to have in place as we grow old. He also talked about the kind of legacy we'd like to leave and the investment we can make in coming generations.

His wife, Margaret, was the guest expert for our first class and the friend who gave me the title for this book and the inspiration that went with it. She helped me start on my victory lap. Thanks to her, I'm progressing from embarrassment and weakness to confidence and strength, from a sense of failure and of my life being over to a greater sense of self-worth and a new appreciation for God's blessings, including His gift of a victory lap.

My legacy is a legacy of stories about my family, about other people, about God, and His dealings with us all.

Mine is a legacy of material belongings that may have little actual value, but are valuable to me because of the people I loved that they belonged to and that I hope will be valuable to my children because of their value to me.

My legacy is a legacy of ideas, of ways of teaching my children, the children and adults I've taught in Bible classes, seminars and lectureships over the years, and the children and adults I've tutored and worked with on subjects from math and grammar to science and history.

As I run my victory lap, I think back over the joys of my life and pray that my family and friends will know the satisfaction I've enjoyed. I pray that my influence will live on in the lives of those I've helped and encouraged as they help and encourage others. And I pray that the mementos, stories and traditions as well as the faith I've received from those who came before me will be valued by those who follow. This is my prayer, and this is my legacy.

Discussion Questions

1. What is a legacy? What does it mean to say you can't help leaving a legacy of some sort?

2. What are some of the legacies people you've known have left?

3. Have you made any plans for distributing your belongings?

4. Why is it important to have a will?

5. What kind of legacy would you like to leave? Money? Ideas?

6. How can you invest in a younger generation?

Bible Study

1. Dorcas was always doing _____ and helping
   the _____(Acts 9:36). When she died, "All the
   _____ stood around him, _____
   and showing him the _____ and other
   _____ Dorcas had made while she was still with
   them (Acts 9:39).

2. Jesus said of the woman with the alabaster jar, "I tell you the
   _____, wherever the _____ is
   preached throughout the _____, what she has done will
   also be told, in _____ of her."(Mark 14:9).

3. [Jesus] took bread, gave thanks and broke it, and gave it to them,
   saying This is my _____ given for you, _____ this in
   _____ of me" (Luke 22:19).

4. "If you want to be _____, go, sell your
   _____ and give to the
   _____, and you will have _____ in
   _____" (Matthew 19:21).

5. "But God said to him, 'You _____! This very _____
   your _____ will be demanded from you. Then who
   will _____ what you have _____ for
   yourself?" (Luke 12:20).

Write in Your Journal

For what will you be remembered? How would you like to be remembered? What kind of legacy can you begin to leave today? Make notes in your journal about your will, living will, funeral desires, and legacy desires.

Endnotes

30 http://www.harrisinteractive.com/vault/2013_MAWMPressRelease.pdf.

31 http://finance.yahoo.com/blogs/the-exchange/half-americans-set-die-without-193140015.html.

32 http://money.cnn.com/retirement/guide/estateplanning_wills.moneymag/index6.htm.

33 Ibid.

34 http://www.jongordon.com/blog/5-ways-to-leave-a-legacy-2/.

35 http://mariashriver.com/blog/2011/10/what-do-you-want-your-legacy-be/.

Lessons From
Growing Old

What does it mean to grow old? It means wisdom and experience, gray hairs, and a less responsive body. It means giving greater attention to physical, mental, emotional, and spiritual well-being. It means maintaining a support network, staying active and involved in life, preparing for death, and considering the legacy you leave behind.

It also means thinking about the things you've learned through a long life. I can list four of mine with just four words: contentment, compassion, harmony, and integrity. When I shared them with our preacher, he asked if I couldn't make them all start with C's. That's a real preacher's response.

I can't, and I won't. But I still think they're important. *Contentment* is being satisfied with what God has given you, including the number of years you've had, and whatever number you may have to come. It's recognizing that God loves you and provides what's best for you.

I've never made much money, and that may mean that I wouldn't have handled it well if I had. But I've had a rich and satisfying life. I have so many things that I'm beginning to despair of going through them all and leaving them in some sort of order for our children.

I've had wonderful opportunities for learning and growing, intellectually and spiritually. I've enjoyed good health for most of my life. I've enjoyed the love of a wonderful family.

We have a wonderful house. One day, a woman brought me home from church. "What a cute little house!" she said as she drove up in front. It was the biggest house I'd ever lived in. When we first moved in, I got confused a couple of times going from one room to another.

I still love it. I enjoy my little office, which used to be a breakfast room, with its bay window. I enjoy our TV room with its back doors opening onto a large lawn with trees, birds, and squirrels. They're a lot of fun to watch.

Compassion is a quality of Jesus. It's His ability to feel for people who have needs. He not only felt, but He met those needs for food, water, healing, and comfort.

I want to be compassionate with the needy around me. I want to feel some of the pain of hunger, thirst, homelessness, abuse, and prejudice. And I want to do what I can to make things better.

I want to pray with compassion, to seek God's intervention in the tragedies of life in the broader world—like war, famine, and upheaval. I want God's peace, provision, and care to rule.

I am an alto. When I think of music, I don't just think of a tune. I think in terms of a somewhat deeper, richer *harmony*. When I think of age, I want to do the same thing. I want to live in harmony with those numbers that define the years God has given me, the life and experience that are mine. I don't want to take off on some melody of my own. I want to live in harmony with the reality of my life.

I also want to live in harmony with the people around me. I want to promote peace, respect, and love. I won't always agree with the people I care about, but I can give them the freedom God gives me to make my own choices—even to make mistakes.

I also want to live with *integrity*. I want to be honest, to value and speak and write truth. I want a oneness, a unity to my life. I don't want to have a divided mind. I want the way I live to correspond with my profession of faith. I want to be genuine and honest before the world. I want to seek good—not just for me and mine, but for all people everywhere.

Part of living in contentment, compassion, harmony, and integrity has to do with our attitude toward growing old. Growing old is a natural part of living. If we don't die young, we will grow old. And at some point, we will become painfully aware of the fact.

I did when I got sick and had brain surgery, a seizure, and pneumonia. It was the longest I'd been in the hospital in my life. In fact, the only prior hospitalizations had been for a tonsillectomy when I was five, the birth of my children, and a short stay for dehydration.

I have truly been blessed, and I continue to be blessed with this, my victory lap.

I pray that you will find blessings through my experiences and my words, and that you will appreciate and enjoy your own victory lap.

Using This Book
As A Bible Class Curriculum

Each class session began with a prayer and Scripture readings by class members. The person who read the Scripture commented on what it said and what it meant to him or her.

That was followed by a discussion related to the topic of that particular class session.

Each student was given a journal, a bound black-and-white composition book with lined pages. They are inexpensive, and yet they serve as a journal, not just for the class session, but for the student to take home and continue writing in. Students should write their names on the cover, then date each section they write.

There was a suggested topic to write about each week, either in the class itself or as homework that relates to the week's subject.

Finally, I invited what I called a "guest" expert on each topic to sit in on each class, participating in the discussion and suggesting ways to deal constructively with the challenges being considered. If you are a part of a larger congregation, you might be able to find all of your guests from within. If not, search neighboring congregations and relationships to locate guests who would be willing to share.

THE VICTORY LAP –
Growing Old With God

1. What Does It Mean to Grow Old?

Scriptures – Job 12:12; Psalm 92:12-14; Proverbs 16:31; Isaiah 46:3-4; Titus 2:1-5

What is "old" to you?

What was "old" when you were a child?

In your journal, write about an older person from your childhood who had an impact on your life.

Invite a guest expert who can share a healthy view of aging with your class.

2. What Are the Challenges of Retirement?

Scriptures – Exodus 20:8-11; 31:1-11; 2 Samuel 19:34-37; Psalm 71:17-18; 90:10, 13-17; Ecclesiastes 6:3-6; 12:1-7; 1 Corinthians 15:58

What are the challenges of growing old? Physical, mental, emotional, spiritual.

How can you adjust to retirement, unstructured time, and lack of set tasks?

What kind of work have you done?

In your journal, write about your employment history (paid or volunteer).

Invite a guest expert who can share some of the challenges of retirement.

3. How Can We Maintain Our Physical Health?

Scriptures – 1 Timothy 4:8; 1 Corinthians 9:24-27; 2 Timothy 2:5; 4:6-8; 1 Corinthians 6:19-20

Discuss the importance of exercise, food, sleep, and dreams. How might the spiritual affect each of these?

What could you do to bring your physical health into better alignment with God's will?

In your journal, write about your physical health and what you do to maintain it.

Invite a physical trainer to class to share simple exercises that will help keep you fit as you grow older.

4. How Can We Maintain Our Mental Health?

Scriptures – 2 Timothy 1:7; 1 John 2:9-11, 15-17; Hebrews 11:7; Hebrews 13:5-6; Philippians 4:4-9

What is the opposite of fear?

What is the source of power?

How can we overcome anxiety and depression?

In your journal, write about the things that you do to exercise your brain.

Invite a neurologist or someone who can share techniques for keeping the brain sharp as you age.

5. How Can We Maintain Our Emotional Health?

Scriptures – Romans 8:9-11; Galatians 2:20; 5:22-23; Philippians 1:9-11; 4:11-13

What steps can we take to control our emotions?

How can we give more control to God?

Discuss how music or songs might influence our emotions?

In your journal, write about a negative emotion that you sometimes have trouble bringing under control. List three things that you might do to help give God control.

Invite a psychologist or Christian counselor to come to class to share ways to maintain good emotional health.

6. How Can We Maintain Our Spiritual Health?

Scriptures – Psalm 1:1-3; Matthew 5:6; Colossians 1:9-10; 2 Timothy 3:16-17; Hebrews 10:24; 1 Peter 2:1-12

Discuss ways to help maintain your spiritual health.

Is it easier for you to maintain your spiritual health by your self-discipline or with the help of others? Discuss.

In your journal, write about three ways you'd like to deepen your relationship with God and His church.

Invite to class someone whom you consider to be a spiritual prayer warrior. Have them share some things they do to stay close to God.

7. How Can We Maintain a Support Network?

Scriptures – Ecclesiastes 4:9-12; Ephesians 4:11-16; 1 Thessalonians 3:2; Hebrews 3:12-13; 10:19-25

Who in your life lifts your spirit and gives you encouragement? Share how they are able to accomplish that.

How can you be an encourager to someone else?

In your journal, write a thank-you note to someone who has encouraged you. Write the name of a person you know who needs encouragement now. Write down two or three things that you might do to encourage that person.

Invite to class a person who exemplifies the encouraging attitude. Ask him to share some simple ways that we can become better encouragers of our friends and family.

8. How Can We Stay Active and Involved?

Scriptures – 1 Thessalonians, 5:12-18; proverbs 24:27; 26:13; Ecclesiastes 11:6; Proverbs 6:9-10; Psalm 104:19-23

What activities bring you joy and satisfaction? How did you discover this activity?

In your journal, write down several new activities that you think would interest you. Make a plan for getting involved in them.

Invite an occupational or physical therapist to class to share how certain activities help keep the body healthy.

9. How can We Prepare for Death?

Scriptures – Psalm 23:4-6; John 14:1-6; 1 Corinthians 15:51-57; Romans 8:38-39; Philippians 1:21-26; 1 Thessalonians 4:13-18; Revelation 2:7,11,17,26-29; 3:5-6, 11-13, 21-22

When were you baptized? What was the setting?

In what situations in life have you been driven to a deeper trust in God?

In what ways has God proven Himself to be faithful in your life?

In your journal, write about your confidence in death and how this connects to your past experiences with God.

Invite to class a hospital chaplain or hospice worker. Have them share some of the different experiences they have had as they help people face death.

10. What Is Your Legacy?

Scriptures – 1 Corinthians 15:58; Philippians 1:21-26

Have you made specific plans for distributing your belongings?

What kind of legacy would you like to leave?

How can you invest in the younger generation?

In your journal, write down the ideal way you would like to be remembered. What steps are you taking now to help that legacy be a reality? Write down any funeral plans and wishes that should be a part of your will.

Invite to class someone who will leave a great legacy through family or contributions. Have them share how they prepared for that.